PRAISE FOR *INVITATION TO SOLITUDE AND SILENCE*

"Ruth Haley Barton has gifted us with a vital way to deeper intimacy with God and our own true self in God through the neglected disciplines of solitude and silence. Along with her own honest biographical witness, she offers us a variety of concrete practices that can help the reader enter solitude and silence with greater ease and understanding of the ways God is present for us in such times, often in the face of our resistances. What she has given us can contribute significantly to a more mature and full spiritual life. She convincingly shows us the vital spiritual importance of an intentional rhythm of work and rest, solitude and community, silence and word."

TILDEN EDWARDS, FOUNDER AND SENIOR FELLOW, SHALEM INSTITUTE FOR SPIRITUAL FORMATION

"I find books in the genre of the contemplative life are often written by mystics who occupy some rarified, ethereal realm in which I don't seem to live. Not so with Ruth Haley Barton's *Invitation to Solitude and Silence*. Ruth takes us on her journey into solitude and silence as one, like most of us, who must learn to commune with God in the muchness of life."

GREG OGDEN, AUTHOR OF *DISCIPLESHIP ESSENTIALS* AND EXECUTIVE PASTOR OF DISCIPLESHIP, CHRIST CHURCH OF OAK BROOK

Invitation to
Solitude and Silence

EXPERIENCING GOD'S

TRANSFORMING PRESENCE

RUTH HALEY BARTON
Foreword by Dallas Willard

InterVarsity Press
Downers Grove, Illinois

InterVarsity Press
P.O. Box 1400, Downers Grove, IL 60515-1426
World Wide Web: www.ivpress.com
E-mail: mail@ivpress.com

InterVarsity Press® is the book-publishing division of InterVarsity Christian Fellowship/USA®, a student movement active on campus at hundreds of universities, colleges and schools of nursing in the United States of America, and a member movement of the International Fellowship of Evangelical Students. For information about local and regional activities, write Public Relations Dept., InterVarsity Christian Fellowship/USA, 6400 Schroeder Rd., P.O. Box 7895, Madison, WI 53707-7895, or visit the IVCF website at <www.ivcf.org>.

Scripture is taken from the New Revised Standard Version of the Bible, *copyright 1989 by the Division of Christian Education of the National Council of the Churches of Christ in the USA. Used by permission.*

Cover design: Cindy Kiple

Cover image: Gary Braasch/Getty Images

ISBN 0-8308-2386-7

Printed in the United States of America ∞

Library of Congress Cataloging-in-Publication Data

Barton, R. Ruth, 1960-
   Invitation to solitude and silence: experiencing God's transforming
presence / Ruth Haley Barton.
       p. cm.
Includes bibliographical references (p.   ).
   ISBN 0-8308-2386-7
   1. Spirituality. 2. Spiritual life—Christianity. 3.
Silence—Religious aspects—Christianity. 4. Solitude—Religious
aspects—Christianity. I. Title.
   BV4501.3.B38 2004
   248.4'7—dc22

                                                                                    2003020593

P	17	16	15	14	13	12	11	10	9	8	7	6
Y	15	14	13	12	11	10	09	08	07	06	05	

To those who have allowed me the privilege of accompanying them on their journey into solitude and silence.

Your faces, your questions and your longings kept me faithful to the challenge of putting into words that which is beyond words.

114363

Contents

Foreword

Blaise Pascal, the remarkable scientist, theologian and Christian of the seventeenth century, remarked in his *Pensees* (section 136) that "all the unhappiness of men arises from one single fact, that they cannot stay quietly in their own room." The reason for this inability, he found, is "the natural poverty of our feeble and mortal condition, so miserable that nothing can comfort us when we think of it closely." In order not to "think of it closely," we turn to what Pascal calls "diversion" to distract us from ourselves:

> Hence it comes people so much love noise and stir; hence it comes that the prison is so horrible a punishment; hence it comes that the pleasure of solitude is a thing incomprehensible.

Pascal also observes that we have "another secret instinct, a remnant of the greatness of our original nature, which teaches that happiness in reality consists only in rest, and not in being stirred up." This instinct conflicts with the drive to diversion, and we develop the confused idea that leads people to aim at rest through excitement, "and always to fancy that the satisfaction which they do not have will come to them if, by surmounting whatever difficulties confront them, they can thereby open the door to rest."

Of course it is a fallacy to think that one just needs more time. Unless a deeper solution is found, "more time" will just fill up in the same way as the time we already have. The way to liberation and rest lies through a decision and a practice.

The decision is to release the world and your fate, including your reputation and "success," into the hands of God. This is not a decision to not act at all, though in some situations it may come to that. It is, rather, a decision concerning *how* you will act: you will act in dependence on God. You will not take charge of outcomes. You will do your part, of course, but your part will always be chastened by a sense of who is God—not you!

A decision to release the world and our fate to God runs contrary to everything within and around us. We have been had by a system of behavior that was here before we were and seeps into every pore of our being. "Sin," Paul tells us, "was in the world," even before the law came. It forms us internally and pressures us externally. Hence we must learn to choose things that meet with God's actions of grace to break us out of the system. These things are the disciplines of life in the Spirit, well known from Christian history but much avoided and misunderstood. For those who do not understand our desperate situation, these disciplines look strange or even harmful. But they are absolutely necessary for those who would find rest for their soul in God and not live the distracted existence Pascal so accurately portrays.

Solitude and silence are the most radical of the spiritual disciplines because they most directly attack the sources of human misery and wrongdoing. To be in solitude is to choose to do nothing. For extensive periods of time. All accomplishment is given up. Silence is required to complete solitude, for until we enter quietness, the world still lays hold of us. When we go into solitude and silence we stop making demands on God. It is enough that God is God and we are his. We learn we have a soul, that God is here, that this world is "my Father's world."

This knowledge of God progressively replaces the rabid busyness and self-importance that drives most human beings, including the religious ones. It comes to possess us no matter where we are. Now, "Whatever we do, in word or deed, we do in the name of the Lord Jesus, giving thanks to God the Father through him" (Col 3:17). Solitude and silence are not another job. They are not, really, something we have to think to do. They are whom we have become. We still need to cultivate solitude and silence, from time to time going alone and being quiet. But we carry them with us wherever we go.

In the contemporary context (especially the religious context) someone needs to tell us about solitude and silence—just to let us know there are such things. Someone then needs to tell us it's okay to enter them. Someone needs to tell us how to do it, what will happen when we do, and how we go on from there. For Ruth Barton that someone was her spiritual director. Now Ruth tells you.

If you would really like to know the "rest appropriate for the people of God" (Heb 4:9), then make the decision to leave all outcomes to God and enter the practice of solitude and silence with Ruth Barton as your guide. As you do so, call upon Jesus to be with you, and trust him. Eventually you will come to know the "rest unto your souls" promised by him who is meek and lowly of heart. It will become the easy and unshakeable foundation for your life and your death.

Dallas Willard

Gratitudes

At times the strength of spiritual community lies in the love of people who refrain from getting caught in the trap of trying to fix everything for us, who pray for us and allow us the pain of our wilderness, our wants, so that we may be more deeply grounded in God.

ROSEMARY DOUGHERTY

Although the journey into solitude and silence is a solitary one, we take the journey within a larger community of those who have gone before and those who share the journey with us now. These are the ones who support us in saying yes to God's invitations in our lives. They are the ones who cheer us on. They faithfully release us to God and then receive us back into their company with reverence and attention to whatever has been received from God in that solitary place. To these companions on the journey I wish to express my gratitude.

To the communities of The Transforming Center. I am deeply grateful for the opportunity to grapple with the challenge of holding silence and space for God in the context of our life and ministry together. I am moved by the ways in which we are learning to honor and trust silence as a means of opening ourselves to God, to each other and to the gift of discernment. We are living some of the great paradoxes of the spiritual life, that when we choose to spend time alone we are somehow better when we are together. When we choose time for silence our words become more meaningful. When we choose to wait, more is accomplished.

To Joe Sherman, faithful friend, trusted agent and ministry partner. Thank you for asking the brave question that began to invite a truer voice to emerge in my writing. Thank you for all the times you have called for that voice along the way. Thank you for your unwavering faith in me. At pivotal times in my life, God has used you to impart courage and confidence and I am deeply grateful.

To Brenda Salter-McNeil, dearest soul sister. We have supported each other on the journey into solitude and silence even when the demands of ministry and leadership, home and family, and our own inner compulsions have made it seem nearly impossible. We have reverenced the things that God has said to us in the quietness and have witnessed the salvation that comes when we wait for God and God alone. Thanks be to God.

To Christine Anderson. Your faithful contributions to my development as an author have been invaluable—the perfect blend of kindness and tact, truth and challenge. Your coaching has pushed me to work harder and with greater levels of realism and professional expertise than I would have otherwise aspired to.

To Bob Fryling, Cindy Bunch and Jeff Crosby at InterVarsity Press. Each of you has contributed your expertise, your confidence and your encouragement in times and ways that have been deeply meaningful. It is a privilege to work in partnership with those who are so personally committed to the rigors of the spiritual journey.

To Sis, the spiritual director who first helped me to see myself as the jar of river water all shaken up and then guided me into the practices that would allow the swirling sediment in my soul to settle. The journey begun that day continues to this very moment.

To friends and loved ones who have watched and prayed for me throughout the writing of this book, particularly my parents, Charles and JoAnn Haley; my brothers, Jonathan Taylor Haley and Bill Haley; and my friends Cindra Stackhouse-Taeztsch, Sheryl Fleisher, Marilyn Stewart and Adele Calhoun.

To Chris, Charity, Bethany and Haley. We have come a long way since those days when we explained my forays into solitude and silence by saying, "Mommy will be a better mommy if she has some time alone with God." Thank you for being patient as I have struggled to learn how to carve out time for quiet in the midst of the fullness of family life. Your willingness to let me go and then come back has been a great gift.

My whole heart rises up in thankfulness.

Ruth Haley Barton

Introduction

To fill a book with words on moving *beyond words* into solitude and silence is a daunting task; it is laughable really, once one sees the irony. I have found myself alternately drawn to the task and strangely resistant.

On the one hand, I have been drawn to the task because my journey into solitude and silence has been the single most meaningful aspect of my spiritual life to date—a pretty strong statement for one who has been a Christian since she was four years old!

On the other hand, solitude and silence represent a continuing challenge for me. Though it has been well over ten years since I first said yes to God's invitation to enter more intentionally into these disciplines, I still find it challenging to protect space for these times apart which satisfy the deep empty places of my soul. Like you, I wrestle with the influences of the secular culture and even religious subcultures that in overt or subtle ways devalue nonproductive times for being rather than doing. And I struggle to trust myself to the mystery that is God in the silent places beyond all the things I think I should know. By now I know better than to blame my struggle on forces "out there." I am more aware than ever that I have my own in-

ner demons that are easily enticed—demons of desire to perform, to
be seen as competent (at least!), productive, culturally relevant, bal-
anced. I still battle these demons regularly when it is time to enter
into these important disciplines.

But what a delight to keep experiencing God's invitations amidst
all the challenges! And what a joy to notice that more and more the
delight is overpowering the demons. For it is a wonderful thing to
be invited. Not coerced or manipulated, but truly invited to the
home of someone you have looked forward to getting to know, to a
party with fun people, on a date with someone who is intriguing.
There is something about being invited that makes the heart glad.
Someone is seeking me out, desiring my presence enough to initiate
an encounter.

The invitation to solitude and silence is just that. It is an invitation
to enter more deeply into the intimacy of relationship with the One
who waits just outside the noise and busyness of our lives. It is an invitation to communication and communion with the One who is always present even when our awareness has been dulled by
distraction. It is an invitation to the adventure of spiritual transformation in the deepest places of our being, an adventure that will result in greater freedom and authenticity and surrender to God than
we have yet experienced.

God's invitation is a winsome one, but it is not casual; it is an invitation from his very heart to the depths of our being. It warrants
serious consideration because it is an invitation to a journey, a quest
really, for something we have been longing for all our lives. Unlike
a trip designed to get us somewhere as efficiently as possible, a
quest requires us to leave familiar dwelling places for strange lands
we cannot yet envision, without knowing when we will return. This
journey requires a willingness to say goodbye to life as we know it

because our heart is longing for something more.

When we embark on such a journey, we understand there will be challenges along the way, unexpected encounters that stretch us to our limits and change the shape of who we are. We know we will emerge changed, bearing the marks of the journey on our soul and body. Our friends may not recognize us when we return; we may not even recognize ourselves!

Such a journey requires commitment—willingness to press on through sunlit days and dark nights, unspeakable beauty and terrible danger, sometimes finding companionship and sometimes feeling utterly alone, sometimes sure we are headed in the right direction, other times afraid we have completely lost our way. It is that perilous and priceless journey inward to that place at the center of ourselves where God dwells.

My guess is that because you have this book in your hand, you are already sensing God's invitation to solitude and silence and a longing to say yes is stirring within you. This book offers spiritual guidance for your journey, helping you to hear God's invitation more clearly and giving you concrete ways of saying yes. Each chapter offers teaching and reflection on different aspects of the journey, but more important, there are practices that will help you to actually enter into solitude and silence. The practices are very simple, but don't be deceived: many of them involve significant paradigm shifts, and we need practice to actually make the shifts.

If you are the type that can't help reading through a book quickly in one sitting, go ahead and do that, but I encourage you then to go back through it, spending time with each reflection and the practice that follows. In fact, it would be best to stay with each chapter and engage the practice until God releases you and indicates you are ready to move on.

This book also offers perspective on what you might experience at different points along the way. There have been several times in my own journey when I thought I was falling off the spiritual path and I needed someone to tell me, "This is what it's like. You haven't fallen off the path, you are right in the heart of the journey." It is this kind of reassurance I want to offer, so you don't give up too soon!

The prophet Elijah, whose journey into solitude and silence has been deeply reassuring to me along the way, serves as a biblical companion throughout this book. There is a difference between reading a story and living in a story, and I have lived in Elijah's story for a very long time. When I began my journey into solitude and silence, it was so challenging and so far outside of my Christian experience that I needed a place in Scripture to land. I needed Scripture that would show me (not just tell me) that I was not alone in what I was experiencing and that the invitation to move from the known into the unknown was a trustworthy one. The concreteness, the humanness and the detail of Elijah's process of moving into solitude and silence grounded me in spiritual reality when it felt as if the foundations of my life were being shaken to the core. Because Elijah's story has informed my own journey so powerfully, I invite you into Elijah's story as well, not so much to gain information as to allow you a place to settle in Scripture when your questions are swirling.

You might wonder why this book is about solitude and silence rather than solitude and Scripture, or solitude and prayer, or solitude and journaling. All of these elements of the spiritual life find their way into the book in different places, but I have chosen to write about solitude and silence because I believe silence is the most challenging, the most needed and the least experienced spiritual discipline among evangelical Christians today. It is much easier to talk about it and read about it than to actually become quiet. We are a very busy, wordy and heady faith tradition. Yet we are desperate to find ways to open ourselves to our God who is, in the end, beyond all of our human constructs and human agendas. With all of our emphasis on theology and Word, cognition and service—and as important as these are—we are starved for mystery, to know this God as One who is totally Other and to experience reverence in his presence. We are starved for intimacy, to see and feel and know God in the very cells of our being. We are starved for rest, to know God beyond what we can do for him. We are starved for quiet, to hear the sound of sheer silence that is the presence of God himself.

The invitation to solitude and silence is an invitation to all of this, and the beauty of an invitation is that we really do have a choice. We can say yes or no. God extends the invitation, but he honors our freedom and will not shove in where he is not wanted. Instead, he waits for us to respond from the depths of our desire. When your invitation comes, I pray you will say yes.

Ahab told Jezebel all that Elijah had done, and how he had killed all the prophets with the sword. Then Jezebel sent a messenger to Elijah, saying, "So may the gods do to me, and more also, if I do not make your life like the life of one of them by this time tomorrow." Then he was afraid; he got up and fled for his life, and came to Beer-sheba, which belongs to Judah; he left his servant there.

But he himself went a day's journey into the wilderness, and came and sat down under a solitary broom tree. He asked that he might die: "It is enough; now, O Lord, take away my life, for I am no better than my ancestors." Then he lay down under the broom tree and fell asleep. Suddenly an angel touched him and said to him, "Get up and eat." He looked, and there at his head was a cake baked on hot stones, and a jar of water. He ate and drank, and lay down again. The angel of the Lord came a second time, touched him, and said, "Get up and eat, otherwise the journey will be too much for you." He got up, and ate and drank; then he went in the strength of that food forty days and forty nights to Horeb the mount of God. At that place he came to a cave, and spent the night there.

Then the word of the Lord came to him, saying, "What are you doing here, Elijah?" He answered, "I have been very zealous for the Lord, the God of hosts; for the Israelites have forsaken your covenant, thrown down your altars, and killed *your prophets with the sword. I alone am left, and they are seeking my life, to take it away."*

He said, "Go out and stand on the mountain before the LORD, for the LORD is about to pass by." Now there was a great wind, so strong that it was splitting mountains and breaking rocks in pieces before the LORD, but the LORD was not in the wind; and after the wind an earthquake, but the LORD was not in the earthquake; and after the earthquake a fire, but the LORD was not in the fire; and after the fire a sound of sheer silence. When Elijah heard it, he wrapped his face in his mantle and went out and stood at the entrance of the cave. Then there came a voice to him that said, "What are you doing here, Elijah?" He answered, "I have been very zealous for the LORD, the God of hosts; for the Israelites have forsaken your covenant, thrown down your altars, and killed your prophets with the sword. I alone am left, and they are seeking my life, to take it away." Then the LORD said to him, "Go, return on your way to the wilderness of Damascus; when you arrive, you shall anoint Hazael as king over Aram . . . and you shall anoint Elisha son of Shaphat of Abel-meholah as prophet in your place. . . ."

So he set out from there, and found Elisha . . . and threw his mantle over him.

1 KINGS 19:1-19

1

Beyond Words

A good journey begins with knowing where we are and being willing to go somewhere else.

RICHARD ROHR

Truth be told, it was desperation that first propelled me into solitude and silence. I wish I could say that it was for loftier reasons, pure desire for God or some such thing. But in the beginning it was desperation, plain and simple. There were things that needed fixing in my life, longings that were painfully unmet, and I had tried everything I knew to fix what was broken and to fill what was lacking, but to no avail.

A grown-up pastor's kid in my early thirties, I was married with three young children of my own, on staff at a church I loved, just beginning to respond to invitations to write and engage in a bit of public speaking. Seminary study rounded out a life that was full and challenging; it demanded all of the energy, focus and priority management I could muster. But inside my soul there was another level of truth that needed to be told, and desperation was probably the only force compelling enough to make me willing to listen.

In the midst of the outward busyness of my life there was an inner chaos that was far more disconcerting. It was particularly alarming to realize that even though I had been a Christian for many years, I was struggling with some of the basics of the spiritual life. For one thing, I could not seem to consistently love my husband and children; elements of selfishness and self-centeredness were being exposed in the crucible of marriage and parenting and were frightening to acknowledge. At best I was impatient with the demands of life in the company of others; at worst I was angry that people wouldn't just leave me alone to pursue my own dreams and ambitions.

At first I trivialized my struggle by categorizing it as a sort of early midlife crisis. But the deeper truth was this: even though I had been a Christian for many years I did not know how to love—really. Particularly when love was demanding or inconvenient or interfered with my own desires, I did not know how to die to myself in even the smallest way. True transformation in the places that really counted seemed just beyond my reach. I was beginning to wonder whether some of the core promises of the Christian life were true at all.

As it turned out, my limited capacity to love was just the tip of an iceberg. There were enormous questions right under the surface of my busy life, questions that I could no longer quiet. There were questions about identity and calling: Was there anything truer about me than the externals of gender-related roles and responsibilities? Was there anything more defining than how hard I could work, the level of excellence I could achieve and other people's assessment of that? There were questions about the possibility of true spiritual transformation: What about those stuck places I was just beginning to acknowledge—those places where I could not break free to love? Was there any power effective enough to touch those intractable places here and now, or was my best hope for transformation some distant possibility beyond the grave? And there were questions about what was lurking deep in the subterranean levels of the soul: What was motivating the frenetic quality of my life and schedule? Why did I find it terribly hard to say no, even when my overcommitment hurt those closest to me? Would I come to the end of my life only to mourn poor choices that did not reflect what is most to be prized?

These were painful questions indeed, and attending to them stirred up emotions I had somehow managed to bury: pockets of anger about past pains and present injustices that covered deep wells of sadness. Waves of confusion about things I used to be so sure of. Undercurrents of loneliness and longing for more. But more of what— God, love, belonging, peace? I wasn't really sure how to name or articulate my longings, but they threatened to pull me into a powerful undertow. I was afraid that if I walked all the way into the emotions and questions that I had worked so hard to ignore and avoid, I might be overtaken. Perhaps my anger would cause me to lash out in ways unbecoming to a Christian. Maybe my sadness would be completely debilitating and I would be unable to pull myself out of it. Perhaps my confusion would make it impossible to teach with conviction. Maybe my loneliness would cause me to search for connection in the wrong ways and in the wrong places.

The more I tried to suppress my emotions and questions and the harder I worked to resist them or pretend they didn't exist, the more they seemed to wield a subterranean power over me. In the midst of much outward productivity, the interior spaces of my life resonated with words like, "There has to be more to the spiritual life than this." Sometimes the words were quiet and wistful, full of a profound sadness. At other times they were feisty, fighting words full of a lack of acceptance: "*This can't be all there is!* And if it is, I'm not sure I want it!" Sometimes there were no words at all—just longings.

What does one do with such an unwieldy hunger? How does one attend to the heart's desperate longing for God in the midst of so much religious activity? What do you do when all the familiar methods for seeking God come up empty? Where does a Christian leader go to articulate questions that seem dangerous and almost sacrilegious? This was *not* a good time to admit to any kind of spiritual emptiness or acknowledge any kind of serious questions about my faith. It was a time for being "good," for being available when people called, for maintaining outward evidences of spiritual maturity and commitment commensurate with the opportunities that were coming my way. And yet these interior groanings were real and needed attention.

Help came through a spiritual director—someone who was more experienced in the ways of the soul, more practiced at recognizing God's invitations in the life of another and willing to support them in making a faithful response. Our paths first crossed because she was a psychologist. I sought her out for therapy because I assumed that my problems were psychological in nature and could be fixed on that level.

Psychological insight and process were indeed valuable—to a point. Eventually, however, she observed that what I needed was spiritual direction and asked if I would be willing for us to shift the focus of our times together to my relationship with God and the invitation to spiritual transformation contained within the questions that I was raising. I had never heard of spiritual direction, but I trusted her to know what was best. So we made the shift.

As we entered into this new kind of relationship, I expected that the answers would continue to come primarily through verbal exchange. I was hoping for advice and a quick fix—in three easy steps if possible! Now, rather than doing psychological talking, we would do spiritual talking. And we did do some talking, but eventually this wise woman said to me, "Ruth, you are like a jar of river water all shaken up. What you need is to sit still long enough that the sediment can settle and the water can become clear."

I couldn't even imagine what it would be like to be still long enough for anything to settle! I couldn't imagine not having an agenda or a prayer list or a study plan. After all, even methods that don't work are better than no methods at all! I couldn't imagine not using words—whether spoken or only formed in my mind. After all, I am a word person. My life as a writer and speaker revolves around being able to make sense out of things by putting them into words. If something couldn't be put into words or processed with words or solved with words, what good could it be?

Last but not least, I couldn't imagine letting go of my own efforts to fix and solve and make progress in my spiritual life. After all, I am an achiever. I had been working at things so hard for so long that such seemingly nonproductive "activity" as sitting alone in silence was completely outside of my normal categories.

But even though my mind had a hard time grasping what this settling would actually be like, the image of the jar of river water captured what I knew to be true about myself. I could not avoid the realization that I *was* the jar of river water all shaken up and the sediment that swirled inside the jar was the busyness, the emotions, the thoughts, the inner wrestlings I had not been able to control. It was a moment of self-discovery—which is where all good spiritual journeying begins.

The image of the jar of river water helped me identify where I was, but it also captured my longing and desire to go somewhere else. To be still long enough so the swirling sediment could settle, the waters of my soul could become clear, and I could see whatever it was that needed to be seen . . . well, that image called to me with the hope of peace, clarity and a deeper level of certainty in God than I had yet known. In the desire this image stirred up, I recognized an invitation to *be still and know* beyond my addiction to noise, words, people and performance-oriented activity. It captured my desire for something more and different, something beyond the head knowledge that no longer sustained my soul.

But still, it was not an easy invitation to accept. Even though it seemed as if all I had known of spiritual life had become a yawning, empty cavity, I didn't like the fact that the only invitation I was getting was an invitation into more nothingness! What was I supposed to do with *that?* What I learned is that you stay with the feelings of desperation and let desperation do its good work.

As strange as it may sound, desperation is a really good thing in the spiritual life. Desperation causes us to be open to radical solutions, willing to take all manner of risk in order to find what we are looking for. Desperate ones seek with an all-consuming intensity, for they know that their life depends on it. Like the cancer patient who travels to a foreign country in the quest for cures that can't be found in familiar territory, spiritual seekers embark on a quest for that which cannot be found within the borders of life as we know it. We embark on a search for healing that has not been found in all the other cures we have tried. We have run all the way to the edges of our own answers; we have exhausted the possibilities and are now finally ready to admit our powerlessness in the face of the great unfixables of life.

∽

Although my spiritual director did not use the terms *solitude* and *silence* to identify the practices she sensed God was inviting me into, I know now that she was encouraging the use of two classic practices spiritual seekers have used through the ages to open themselves to knowing and hearing God more deeply. Solitude and silence are not self-indulgent exercises for times when an overcrowded soul needs a little time to itself. Rather, they are concrete ways of opening to the presence of God beyond human effort and beyond the human constructs that cannot fully contain the Divine.

The practices of solitude and silence are radical because they challenge us on every level of our existence. They challenge us on the level of culture: there is little in Western culture that supports us in entering into what feels like unproductive time for being (beyond human effort) and listening (beyond human thought). They confront us on the level of our human relationships: they call us away from those relationships for a time so we can give undivided attention to God. They challenge us on the level of our soul: in the silence we become aware of inner dynamics we have been able to avoid by keeping ourselves noisy and busy. They draw us into spiritual battle: in silence there is the potential for each of us to "know that I am God" with such certainty that the competing powers of evil and sin and the ego-self can no longer hold us in their grip. *All the forces of evil band together to prevent our knowing God in this way, because it brings to an end the dominion of those powers in our lives.*

Looking back on my own beginnings with solitude and silence, I know that without desperation I would have been much less willing to face these challenges. I doubt I would have been willing to enter into such unfamiliar territory—the silent places of the soul where one is not sure what one will find, the risky quest for God beyond wordy prayers and content-laden sermons and Bible studies—and stay there long enough for the waters of my soul to become clear. Without the desire for something more, I probably would have just kept on doing what I was doing. I needed to let the twin engines of desperation and desire lift me out of my stuck places into the realm where the spiritual life happens at God's initiative rather than the pushing and forcing that often characterizes my effort.

Perhaps you sense the same thing in yourself—something like desperation or desire that is creating a willingness to move beyond the familiar into uncharted territory. Pay attention to these stirrings of the soul. Rather than running from them, distracting yourself from them or suppressing them, let the dynamics of desperation and desire do the good work of inviting you deeper into solitude and silence where the presence of God makes itself known beyond words.

> *When we make room for silence we make room for ourselves. . . . Silence invites the unknown, the untamed, the wild, the shy, the unfathomable—that which rarely has a chance to surface within us.*
>
> GUNILLA NORRIS, *SHARING SILENCE*

This is exactly what Elijah did. Elijah had just experienced great success, but Jezebel, the queen of Israel, was so threatened by the power of his prophetic ministry that she threatened to kill him. This sent Elijah over the edge of fear and depression, and he ran for his life. Eventually he withdrew even from his personal servant and walked unto the wilderness until he collapsed under a solitary broom tree, so discouraged that he told God that he might as well take his life.

Eventually, Elijah's willingness to enter into solitude and silence opened room for God to minister to him in ways he had not yet experienced. Here he had the opportunity to face himself, to give up control of his own journey and to experience God's transforming presence.

Rest assured that as you take your place under the solitary broom tree in the wilderness of your own doubts, questions and unfulfilled longings, you are in good company. Elijah and countless spiritual seekers after him have experienced God's presence in solitude and silence as they have pulled back from the noisy, peopled places of their lives. Here we sit our souls down and wait for that which comes from beyond ourselves. Here we give in to desperation and desire until God comes to us and does for us what we cannot do for ourselves.

Practice

Settle into a comfortable physical position and take three deep breaths—inhale deeply and exhale slowly. As you breathe and become quiet, allow that which is usually unknown and unnamed within you to surface. Notice the dynamics that are drawing you deeper into solitude and silence at this time in your life. What is happening inside you and in your relationship with God right now that seems to be inviting you into solitude and silence? Do the words *desperation* and *desire* capture what you are experiencing, or is there another word or phrase that more accurately expresses what is going on in your interior world?

Allow these inner experiences and dynamics to come to the surface; feel them, name them, sit with them, express them to God if you wish. Today, let it be enough to create space for yourself and those things that are stirring in the interior places of your soul. Listen to them not as experiences to be avoided but as invitations to open yourself to God in new ways. When your time allotted for silence is over, thank God for his presence with you during this time of noticing.

2

Beginnings

> Without solitude it is virtually impossible to live a spiritual life.
> . . . We do not take the spiritual life seriously if we do not
> set aside some time to be with God and listen to him.
>
> HENRI NOUWEN

To enter into solitude and silence is to take the spiritual life seriously. It is to take seriously our need to quiet the noise of our lives, to cease the constant striving of human effort, to pull away from our absorption in human relationships *for a time* in order to give God our undivided attention. In solitude God begins to free us from our bondage to human expectations, for there we experience God as our ultimate reality—the One in whom we live and move and have our being. In solitude our thoughts and our mind, our will and our desires are reoriented Godward so we become less and less attracted by external forces and can be more deeply responsive to God's desire and prayer in us.

Silence deepens the experience of solitude. In silence we not only withdraw from the demands of life in the company of others but also allow the noise of our own thoughts, strivings and compulsions to settle down so we can hear a truer and more reliable Voice. Reliance on our own thoughts and words, even in our praying, can be one facet of a need to control things, to set the agenda, or at least to know what the agenda is even in our relationship with God. It is in silence that we habitually release our own agendas and our need to control and become more willing and able to give ourselves to God's loving initiative. In silence we create space for God's activity rather than filling every minute with our own.

God is infinitely patient. He will not push himself into our lives. He knows the greatest thing he has given us is our freedom. If we want habitually, even exclusively, to operate from the level of our own reason, he will respectfully keep silent. We can fill ourselves with our own thoughts, ideas, images, and feelings.

He will not interfere. But if we invite him with attention, opening the inner spaces with silence, he will speak to our souls, not in words or concepts, but in the mysterious way that Love expresses itself—by presence.

M. Basil Pennington, Centered Living

But silence is not always as easy as it sounds. At least that has been my experience. What sounds like an inspired idea in a spiritual director's office is actually very difficult for those of us who have been moving so fast for so long. In the beginning I felt like a remedial student with special needs for a slower pace and individual tutoring. While "normal" students get to start out with twenty minutes of silence, I needed to begin with a more modest goal of ten minutes a day because that was all I could handle. But no matter; I decided it was better to celebrate small successes than become discouraged by larger failures.

And solitude and silence are not, in the end, about success and failure. They are about showing up and letting God do the rest. They are not an end in themselves; they are merely a *means* through which we regularly make ourselves available to God for the intimacy of relationship and for the work of transformation that only God can accomplish. Richard Foster writes, "Spiritual disciplines are the main way we offer ourselves to God as a living sacrifice. We are doing what we can do with our bodies, our minds, our hearts. God then takes this simple offering of ourselves and does with it what we cannot do, producing within us deeply ingrained habits of peace, love and joy in the Holy Spirit."

Still, how surprising (and humbling!) to find that something so seemingly simple and doable can be so difficult! For the first year or so it seemed like all I did was struggle to make it to the ten-minute mark, all the while noticing the noisiness inside my own head, the pull of distractions, the resistance I felt to this new and challenging practice. Somehow during those moments the need to do laundry seemed more urgent, to-do lists began to compile themselves effortlessly in my head, people and situations I hadn't thought of for years presented themselves unbidden, emotions and questions I usually didn't allow myself to acknowledge took me totally by surprise. The spirit of cynicism whispered, *How pointless is this? We're not getting anything done here!*

But with a little structure and the support of someone who was certain this was what I needed, I was able to stick with it. I began to experience the "spiritual law of gravity" that functions just like the physical law of gravity, and little by little I learned to trust it. When a jar of river water sits still, the law of gravity causes the sediment to eventually settle to the bottom so that the water becomes clear. We don't have to do anything to cause that settling except leave the jar alone for a while. The same is true of the spiritual law of gravity. When we sit quietly in God's presence, the sediment that is swirling in our souls begins to settle. We don't have to do anything but show up and trust the spiritual law of gravity that says, *Be still, and the knowing will come.*

The most important thing about solitude and silence is, at some point, to stop talking about it and reading about it and thinking about and "just do it!" as the Nike commercial admonishes. But a little guidance can be helpful, so I offer you a few ideas to get you started.

First of all, it is important to establish a sacred space—that is, space set apart for God and God alone. Sacred space is *a physical place* that is designated for your times alone with God; it is best for it to be separate from your desk or any other place where you are in work mode. If for some reason you do choose to use your office space, the simple act of turning your chair away from the desk to face a window or sitting on comfortable cushions on the floor can shift your soul's stance from a work mentality to a stance of listening and receiving. You may also want to introduce a physical symbol or religious artifact that speaks to your soul of spiritual reality. For me, lighting a candle is a powerful symbol of the reality of the Holy Spirit present with me in my times of solitude. Ever since the Holy Spirit rested on the heads of the apostles as tongues of fire in Acts 2, the flame has been a Christian symbol of Christ's ongoing presence with us through the Spirit. Others use icons or a cross or items from nature as physical reminders of spiritual reality that help them be present to God in their times of silence.

Sacred space is also *a place in time* set apart to give God our undivided attention. This is a time for resting in God, enjoying his company and allowing intimacy to deepen without any utilitarian purpose. This time is clearly set apart from work or ministry-related activities. Preparations for the Friday night Bible study or the Sunday school lesson you agreed to teach or the sermon you're working on for next Sunday are left for another time.

Over time our body and soul responds to established rhythms, so eventually the very act of entering this set-apart time and place ushers us into our own inner sanctuary. There we can listen to our desire for God and God's desire for us and allow that desire to guide us beyond our information-grasping, controlling, problem-solving patterns of relating into the beyond-words communion we seek.

Sacred space is also *a place in our soul* that is set apart for God and God alone. Especially for those of us who are involved in ministry of any kind, it can be an important discipline to maintain an inner place that is private, shared only between us and God. We might commit ourselves to pondering the things that take place during solitude in our heart, as Mary did, at least for a time, rather than sharing them too quickly or using them immediately as tools for ministry. This is a way of keeping some things precious and sacred rather than allowing them to be commandeered for utilitarian purposes. It reflects the same spirit and intent with which we protect the privacy of our interactions with intimate friends.

Decide ahead of time how much time you will spend in silence. Remember to begin with a modest goal, particularly if solitude and silence are new practices for you. As I discovered, even ten minutes of silence can be very challenging if we are accustomed to a hectic pace of life and have depended heavily on words and activity to express our discipleship. It may take some time to even reach the goal of ten minutes, let alone become comfortable with it. However, it is not the amount of time or the level of difficulty that is important. What is important is that we are faithful to the practice.

As you enter into your time of silence, pay attention to your body and settle into a comfortable yet alert position. You don't want to be distracted by physical discomfort, but you also don't want to fall asleep!

Ask for a simple prayer that expresses the openness and desire for God that you have been experiencing. This prayer is simply a word or phrase that "gathers up" your desire for God and helps you to stay present with it. A simple prayer coupled with a body posture that reflects your heart attitude can be very powerful in helping you to begin waiting expectantly on God.

When I started practicing the discipline of silence, the simplest and truest thing I could say to God was "Here I am." There was much confusion in my soul and

Wordless prayer . . . is humble, simple, lowly, prayer in which we experience our total dependence on God and our awareness that we are in God. Wordless prayer is not an effort to "get anywhere," for we are already there (in God's presence). It is just that we are not sufficiently conscious of our being there.

WILLIAM SHANNON, *SILENCE ON FIRE*

much that was new for me about this way of praying. The only thing I knew for sure was that I wanted to be with God, to be available for whatever he could or would do in my life. The words "Here I am" seemed to best capture my willingness and my desire. Beginning with this simple prayer as I sat with my hands open in my lap helped me to enter into prayer beyond words. It was a concrete expression of my willingness *in the moment* to release whatever agendas I might have in coming to God, to cease striving and receive whatever God wanted to give.

In the years since, other words or phrases like "Come, Lord Jesus" or "Lord Jesus Christ, have mercy on me" or just "Help!" have most accurately captured my need or desire for God in the moment. Sometimes kneeling or lying flat on the floor expresses my heart toward God best. Not only do such simple prayer phrases and physical postures function as an entry point into silence, they also help us remain in a listening posture toward God even in the midst of distraction. When distractions come, it is best not to waste energy on judging ourselves but rather to gently bring ourselves back to our original desire and intent by repeating the prayer word or phrase we have been given.

When the time you have allotted for silence is up (you can use a timer if you wish so you don't have to keep checking the clock), close by expressing gratitude to God, praying in spontaneous words or reciting the Lord's Prayer or some other written prayer.

As you emerge from silence, resist the urge to judge your experience by any kind of utilitarian measure: "I didn't get anything out of it," or "God didn't speak to me," or "I'm awful at this sort of thing!" Remember, the purpose of solitude and silence is just to be with God, to commune with him on that beyond-words level that those who are in love know so well.

Practice

Begin to put the elements in place for incorporating solitude and silence into your life on a regular basis. This may take a few days or even weeks of experimenting and reflecting, so be patient with the process.

1. *Identify your sacred space and time.* Explore all the possibilities for a time and physical space in which you can be alone on a regular basis. Preferably you can identify a spot in your home, outdoors or in your office that helps you to settle into a quiet and receptive state of being. Consider whether there are any spiritual symbols or artifacts you would like to bring into this space to help you to be present to the spiritual reality of God's presence with you. Feel free to experiment,

noticing what works and what doesn't, until you find the best time and place for you. Once you have identified it, you may want to tell family members or roommates about your new commitment, so they can honor the time by not interrupting you and honor the space by staying out of it during your times alone with God.

2. *Begin with a modest goal,* especially if silence is a new practice for you. Ten, fifteen or twenty minutes of time spent in actual silence is realistic, depending on such factors as your personality, pace of life, reliance on words and activity. You can always increase the time as your capacity for silence increases. The amount of time is not nearly as important as the regularity of the practice.

3. *Settle into a comfortable yet alert physical position.* One excellent posture for beginning is to sit in a comfortable straight-backed chair with back and shoulders straight but also relaxed and open, both feet flat on the floor, hands in a comfortable position in your lap. Over time you may choose other prayer postures (see next point), but this is a good place to start.

4. *Ask God to give you a simple prayer that expresses your openness and desire for God.* Choose a prayer phrase that expresses your desire or need for God these days in the simplest terms possible. It is best if the prayer is no more than six or eight syllables so that it can be prayed very naturally in the rhythm of your breathing. Pray this prayer several times as an entry into silence and also as a way of dealing with distractions.

Distractions are inevitable, so when they come, simply let them go by like clouds floating across the sky. Help yourself return to your prayerful intent by repeating the prayer you have chosen. Use your prayer phrase for as long as it captures what is most true about your heart's desire for God, and link it with a body posture that also helps you express your spiritual desire.

5. *Close your time in silence with a prayer of gratitude for God's presence with you, or pray the Lord's Prayer.*

6. *Resist the urge to judge yourself or your experiences in silence.* The purpose of time spent in silence is just to be with God in whatever state you are in and to let him be in control. Trust that whatever your time in silence was like, it was exactly as it should be.

3

Resistance

In silence all of our usual patterns assault us. . . . That is why
most people give up rather quickly. When Jesus was led by
the Spirit into the wilderness, the first things to show up were
the wild beasts.

RICHARD ROHR

In a way, Elijah was fortunate because he was forced into solitude by
his circumstances and life situation. As a prophet in Israel, he had
just performed several miracles, including what was perhaps the cul-
mination of his entire prophetic ministry. In the midst of Israel's apos-
tasy and challenges from pagan priests who had turned away from
God, Elijah had set out to prove that Israel's God was the one true
God. He set up a contest in which the prophets of Baal built an altar
and slaughtered a bull as a sacrifice to their gods. They would then
call to their gods to "answer by fire" and consume the offering, proving that their gods were real.

The prophets of Baal called to their gods all day, but nothing happened. Then Elijah repaired the altar of the Lord, dug a trench around it and placed a bull on it as an offering to the Lord. For good measure, he soaked the altar with water three times until the water ran all around the altar, filling up the trench. Then he cried out to God, and the fire of God descended on the altar, consumed everything on it and around it, "and even licked up the water in the trench."

The people of Israel fell on their faces in God's presence, acknowledging him as the true God. The prophets of Baal tried to run away from such a fearsome display of power, but Elijah captured them and killed them all.

When we catch up with Elijah in 1 Kings 19, he is exhausted from the outpouring of spiritual, physical and emotional energy that this confrontation had required. His life is in danger because of the threat he now posed for the queen of the land, and he is deeply afraid. He is in the throes of the kind of major letdown that often comes when we have given everything we've got. So there was literally *nothing he could do* but collapse under a solitary broom tree.

Most of us are not yet at such a breaking point. We are still fairly functional, trying to keep things under control, full of all sorts of reasons we should remain firmly entrenched in noise and words. The result is that even though we may be quite convinced that solitude is something we need, doubt and resistance often flare up right at the moment when we are about to enter in.

I call this perplexing dynamic "the push-pull phenomenon." It seems no matter how well I understand the necessity of solitude, no matter how much I feel drawn to it, no matter how well I plan for it, there are forces working against it both externally and internally. My entry into solitude often feels like the hard landing of an aircraft that this flight attendant humorously describes: "Ladies and gentlemen, please remain in your seats until Captain Crash and the crew have brought the aircraft to a screeching halt against the gate. And once the tire smoke has cleared and the warning bells are silenced, we'll open the door and you can pick your way through the wreckage to the terminal."

When life is as noisy and fast-paced as mine, it feels as if my approach to solitude involves slamming to a screeching halt. The smoke of clutter and distraction billows around me, and warning bells sound, telling me that I have been in a bit of danger and it's a good thing I'm on the ground. Picking my way through the wreckage of external distractions, I stumble off the plane into the presence of the One who has been waiting for me to arrive, the One who loves me no matter what kind of disheveled shape I am in and is so glad I've made it home.

I try to run into God's arms and give myself to his embrace, but I am holding lots of stuff, and it gets in the way. The baggage I am carrying makes me clumsy and hard to hug. I want to set it down, but where? I want to do something with it, but what?

We all come to solitude holding a lot: cares and concerns about our responsibilities, fear and uncertainty about the experience of solitude itself, longing, and desire. The fact that we are holding so much and don't know what to do with it all can sabotage our efforts to enter in if we don't know how to pay attention and sort it out.

I remember one time when the push-pull dynamic was so strong I just couldn't avoid it. I was sitting at Chicago's O'Hare Airport waiting for a flight to Washington, D.C., where I was scheduled to participate in a five-day quiet retreat. My weary little soul felt more than ready to unplug from the demands of family life, ministry responsibilities and decision making in order to give myself to someone else's spiritual guidance for a time. One aspect of the retreat I felt most drawn to was a thirty-six-hour silent sabbath—quite a departure from the noisy,

overscheduled "retreats" I had been accustomed to. Given the hectic-
ness of my life, it was the silence I was most looking forward to.

What a surprise to discover that even though I had managed to
pull this great plan together, had somehow extricated myself from all
of my responsibilities, had gotten myself to the airport, when I was
about to move into solitude and silence I was ambushed by fear and
concern. First of all, I worried about the relationships and responsibilities I was leaving behind. *Do I really have the right to pull away this
completely to give God my undivided attention? Will everybody survive
without me? What if something major occurs in my daughters' lives and
I'm not around to give what only a mother can give? Will my husband be
able to handle a full-time job along with managing the home front? What
about work? Can I really afford to be so completely out of the loop at such
an important point in my vocational life?* (I was at the tail end of the in-
terviewing process for a job I really wanted, and this trip meant completely disconnecting from that process for five days.) *Will I be
disciplined enough to leave my cell phone off and refuse to check voicemail,
or will I be distracted by the urge to sneak a listen and attend to the urgent
messages? How far behind will I be when I get back?*

As I allowed myself to become aware of these concerns and feel the
anxiety (rather than censoring them), I sensed God gently inviting
me to consider this question: "Will you trust me to care for these
things? Can you trust that I love your family and friends even more
than you do and I will care for them while you are giving this time
and attention to our relationship? Will you trust me to keep working
to bring forth my good intentions in your life without your direct involvement, at least for this little while? Can you accept the fact that
you are not indispensable and allow the world to go on without you
for these few moments?"

I'm glad God was gentle, because otherwise I might have been embarrassed by such obvious questions. It is one thing to read Bible verses about casting our cares on God. It is one thing to sing worship songs that say, "He is able, more than able to accomplish what concerns me today." It is quite another to actually place all those things that we care about so deeply in God's hands for a little while so we can give him our undivided attention.

This letting go is so challenging that many of us need help with it. When I am guiding people into their initial experiences with solitude and silence, I ask them to actually list the cares and concerns weighing on them in the moment on a piece of paper. Then I invite them to place the page in an envelope marked "TRUST" and set the envelope aside as a concrete symbol of giving these things over to God's care as they move into solitude. The concreteness of this act helps them to actually let go of the baggage they have brought with them so they can settle into God's embrace.

Once we place our cares and concerns into God's care, we may be surprised by a more subtle concern: fear of the experience of solitude. This is what surprised me most as I sat in the airport waiting to wing my way to the retreat. Even though I had planned for it so diligently and had had some experience with short periods of solitude and silence, this extended time felt like a risky step into the unknown. I wasn't prepared for the raw fear that ambushed me. Looking for some way to keep myself from being swept away by feelings of panic, I reached for my journal and let my fears flow:

> I've looked forward to this so much . . . but the funny thing now is that I'm scared and uptight about so many things. The biggest fear is about the silence, not knowing if I'll be able to settle down, not knowing what I will have to face within myself.
>
> I'm afraid of being bored, frantic, panicky.

I'm afraid of wanting to go home and not being able to.

I'm afraid of being bored with the people. (I'm already getting glimpses of an addiction to being with exciting people who excite something in me.) I'm afraid of not being able to sleep.

I'm afraid of not getting enough exercise and getting lethargic and depressed.

I'm afraid of hearing promptings from God that are risky to follow.

I'm afraid of letting go and letting my destiny unfold without my direct involvement. I'm afraid of being bored and not having enough to do.

I'm just plain afraid. I can't believe it.

It's not a pretty picture, but that's the way it was. If I hadn't already paid for the flight and checked my bags, I might have turned around and gone home!

Listening to our fears rather than ignoring them can give us a great deal of insight into the conscious and unconscious resistance we have toward solitude and silence. For one thing, solitude and silence leave us without our normal distractions, those things that keep us out of touch with our interior world. On some level the human psyche recognizes that without our normal distractions we might come in touch with realities we are usually able to avoid. As Dallas Willard puts it, "Silence is frightening because it strips us as nothing else does, throwing us upon the stark realities of our life. It reminds us of death, which will cut us off from this world and leave only us and God. And in the quiet, what if there turns out to be very little between us and God?"

Entering into solitude and silence also moves us into a realm where we are not in control. The practice of silence in particular honors the reality that it is God who initiates in the spiritual life; he is the

One who calls it forth in his way and in his time. But even as silence and solitude bring us face to face with our addiction to being in control, there is also an invitation: the invitation to let go and allow God to be in control.

Perhaps the deepest and hardest to articulate fear is the fear that this God whom we cannot control will not meet us in the way we want to be met. Sometimes this expresses itself as a question: "What if I show up and God doesn't? Sure, he showed up for people like Elijah and Moses. And maybe he shows up for those spiritual, mystical types. But what if he doesn't show up for me?" This

God comes like the sun in the morning—when it is time. We must assume an attitude of waiting, accepting the fact that we are creatures and not creator. We must do this because it is not our right to do anything else; the initiative is God's, not ours. We are able to initiate nothing; we are only able to accept."

CARLO CARRETTO, *THE GOD WHO COMES*

fear may present itself in words, or it may be a vague feeling of dread or uncertainty we can't quite name. And so we hesitate at the gateway to solitude and silence, afraid that "this solitude thing works for everybody else, but it won't work for me."

Acknowledging my cares and worries invites me to trust God with what is "out there"; acknowledging this very intimate fear challenges me to trust God with myself, my heart, my soul, my longing and the fear that my longing will not be met. And that's even harder. It brings me to the point all deepening relationships eventually come to: when somebody has to take a leap of faith into the free-fall that is intimacy. This is the point at which we decide that this relationship matters enough and this person is worth putting our heart on the line for. In the vulnerability of love we risk saying, "Here I am. With my whole heart, soul, mind and body I am here, ready and willing to move more deeply into relationship with you. I make myself available to you, and I will wait for you. There is nothing I can do to control the outcomes. There is nothing I can do to force your response or make your response what I want it to be. All I can do is put myself out there and wait." And that is a fearsome place to be, but oh so necessary.

The willingness to name our fear as we enter into solitude opens the way for God to reassure us with his presence, much as the presence of a loving parent comforts a child who wakes trembling with fear in the night. It also enables us—eventually—to peel back the fear, revealing something even truer: our desire for God. This desire is the flip side of our fear. To put it another way, desire is what stirs underneath our fear—desire to be met by God, desire to be touched by God in ways we can feel and know, desire to be given over to God in utter abandonment and trust.

Many of us are not very good at acknowledging our desire. As Christians we tend to be skeptical and suspicious of desire, for it is not easily controlled; experience tells us that desire can be like a quiet little campfire that sparks a forest fire engulfing the whole forest. *What if I let myself feel my desire and it gets out of control? What if I begin to desire things I can't have? How do I live with the pain of unfulfilled desire?*

Depending on our experience of wanting things and then receiving them, or not, we may harbor deep-seated fear that we will not get what our heart desperately wants. It can be frightening to allow ourselves to want something we're not sure we can have, especially if it is something as essential as the presence of God in our lives. In many of us, the fear of not getting what our heart longs for has led us to develop an unconscious pattern of distancing ourselves from our desire in order to avoid the pain of its lack of fulfillment.

But the truth is that desire is the life-blood surging through the heart of the spiritual life. You may not realize it, but your desire for

God is the truest and most essential thing about you. It is truer than your sin, it is truer than your woundedness, it is truer than your net worth, your marital status or any role or responsibility you hold. Your desire for God and your capacity to connect with God as a human soul is the essence of who you are.

But there is an even greater truth: before you were even aware of your desire for God, God desired you. He created you with a desire for him that groans and yearns in the very fiber of your being. We love God because God first loved us. We desire God because God first desired us. We reach for God because he first reached for us and created us with a longing for himself. Right in the very center of our desire for God is God's desire for us, pulsating with love and longing. When we feel our desire, we are actually responding to God, because he has already initiated with us. It might feel as if our desire for God originates with us, but the truth is that the origin of our desire for God is God's desire for us.

When we cut ourselves off from awareness of our desire, we cut ourselves off from the very invitation of God into the intimacy we seek. And so desire, the very human dynamic that often confuses us and muddles our thinking, is a part of what we carry with us as we walk through the gateway to solitude. If we don't know how to attend to it, we may make the mistake of trying to set it aside or minimize it when instead we need to pay

> *One can begin one's quest [for God] by attending to the desires of the heart.*
>
> *The Spirit is revealed in our genuine hopes for ourselves and the world. . . . Desire functions as the fuel that drives the whole journey. . . . How brightly burns the flame of desire for a love affair with God, other persons and the cosmos? Do we know that to desire and seek God is a choice that is always available to us?*
>
> ELIZABETH DREYER, *EARTH CRAMMED WITH HEAVEN*

attention to it. We need to hold it close and fan it into flame so it becomes the guide and the impetus for our spiritual journey.

When we pull back the curtain on our fears and resistance, we are left with our desire—pure, naked, quivering desire—which is the surest guide for the spiritual quest. In the end the human soul will choose what it most wants. If we are brave enough to stay with this experience of wanting something we do not yet have, we discover that underneath all other desire is a desire for God, for love, for the true belonging.

Solitude, then, is all about desire: it is about lovers desiring each other enough to finally take the leap into trust, intimacy, uninhibited expression. It is about friends saying, "I want to be with you so badly that I'll rearrange everything so that we can see each other."

As I listened to my fear and peeled it back on my trip to Washington, and as I settled in, I discovered desire underneath it all. As the time for silence approached I was able to write,

> I am going into it [the silence] with much anticipation. Anticipation of resting and being with God in deep communion, as in settling into extended time with a beloved friend. It feels good to feel that way about the presence of God. . . . The yearning these days is about two things. One is wanting to hear from God. I really want to hear clearly enough so that I can follow wherever. The other, though, is a yearning for release and freedom. I've been in a period of relative freedom, but I realize lately that I've been bound up again by shame, by fear, by drivenness, by attachments, by my addiction to excitement. I take the risks but not freely. I wrestle so much before, during and after. I expend so much emotional and physical energy in that kind of agony. I do so want to be released so I can move through life with a sense of freedom and power and certainty in God in me.

It was desire that became my guide into those days of solitude and silence.

To enter into solitude is to listen to our desire as it calls us deeper into the intimacy our hearts seek. It is to allow our desire—over time—to become concrete, focused, clear. What is your desire saying these days? Are you listening?

Practice

As you enter into solitude and silence today, notice your own experience of the push-pull phenomenon. When have you noticed resistance (pushing you away from solitude) and desire (pulling you toward solitude) functioning within you at the same time? What are you noticing right now?

What cares and concerns do you need to entrust to God's care so you can be fully present with him in solitude? Allow them to surface, along with the emotions surrounding them. Then jot them in your journal or on a separate piece of paper. Release them to God through prayer, or use a symbolic gesture like placing the page in an envelope and setting it aside. Notice how it feels to have a way of releasing care and concern as part of your routine of entering into solitude. You may want to incorporate this into your practice regularly.

Do you notice any fear or anxiety these days about the experience of solitude? When have you been aware that fear sabotages your efforts to enter more deeply into solitude and silence? Use words, phrases, pictures or images to help you express your fear to God. Don't waste energy trying to fight your fear; just let it be in God's presence, like a child who is comforted by a parent's presence when she is frightened. Listen for God's response.

What does your desire feel like, sound like, look like these days?

How easy or difficult is it for you to stay with your experience of desire? Are you brave enough to own your desire, to say it and claim it as the truest thing about you, so that it can take you where your heart has been longing to go? Close your time of silence with a prayer of gratitude for God's presence with you, or pray the Lord's prayer as a way of transitioning to whatever comes next in your day.

4

Dangerously Tired

> Because we do not rest we lose our way. . . . Poisoned by
> the hypnotic belief that good things come only through
> unceasing determination and tireless effort, we can never
> truly rest. And for want of rest our lives are in danger.
>
> WAYNE MULLER

Whether like Elijah you have been driven into solitude by desperation or whether you have entered more willingly, you may be surprised by what happens once you get to a place of silence. You may fall asleep while trying to pray. Perhaps you can't concentrate on the Scripture you're reading. You may find yourself longing to curl up under a blanket and rest, and you try hard to resist your body's need. You may even acknowledge, with some level of disillusionment or cynicism, that solitude doesn't hold any real attraction for you. The idea itself elicits a feeling of weariness, a sense that you are forcing something rather than being drawn in. Solitude feels like just one more thing you *have* to do rather than something you *want* to do.

While your first instinct may be to judge yourself for lack of focus or lack of discipline, it is much better simply to notice what's true and let it be what it is, just as Elijah did.

When Elijah entered into solitude and silence, one of the first things he had to reckon with was how tired and depleted he was on every level. Actually he didn't reckon with it; he just gave in to it. He simply lay down under the broom tree and fell asleep. God did not waste time trying to deal with him intellectually or even spiritually, because it wouldn't have done any good. He began by dealing with Elijah's physical weariness and depletion—he let Elijah sleep. Then he woke Elijah up when it was time to eat and drink, provided food and water for him, told him to go back to sleep, and then started the process all over again.

Elijah's experience has been a great comfort to me along the way, because when I began my journey into solitude and silence I too needed a solitary broom tree where I could give in to my deep-down-to-the-bone tiredness and listen to what it was saying about my life. And I was surprised that one of the first things my spiritual director helped me to attend to was my physical condition. We talked about what I was eating and drinking, how much sleep I was getting, whether I was exercising—many of the same things the angel of the Lord attended to with Elijah.

As it turned out, I needed the same kind of direction Elijah needed for finding ways to rest in God and give him access to those places in me that needed refreshment and care. Like Elijah, I was too tired and worn out to find God—or anything else for that matter. I was frustrated with how hard it was to clear time in my schedule for solitude, ashamed at how often I didn't actually get there even when I'd planned for it, and discouraged by how tired I was when I arrived. During solitude I fought feelings of exhaustion by attempting to do something that felt "productive" like reading my Bible, journaling or meditating on some very profound thought.

Eventually Elijah's story invited me to stop fighting my exhaustion and surrender to it in God's presence. I had to acknowledge that all of my efforts to ignore my tiredness or fight my way through had not provided any lasting solutions. Yes, I could sometimes press on with spurts of energy motivated by a well-developed sense of "I ought to do this" and "I should do that." But the exhaustion and discouragement were always right under the surface of my efforts, threatening to overwhelm me with disillusionment and the temptation to give up. Elijah's experience demonstrated that God was willing to meet me in the midst of such tiredness and disillusionment. In fact, it appeared that a willingness to surrender created the opportunity for God to come in and minister in very practical and personal ways. And so I was inspired to let my exhaustion be what it was and see what God would do.

Fatigue and depletion may be the first thing you need to attend to as well. Rather than being a source of shame or discouragement, your sleepiness or lack of motivation for the journey into solitude may be a symptom of low-level exhaustion. You may be very tired, and when you let down in the quietness of solitude, you become more aware of it. Chances are, you have grown so accustomed to feeling tired that you have actually accepted it as *normal*.

In addition to fatigue itself, there may also be some guilt. You think that if you were better organized or more spiritual, you would not be tired. But times of solitude and silence are not times for judging. They are times for noticing—noticing what is true about us in a given moment and then being in God's presence with the things we've noticed. In this case, solitude is a time for noticing how tired we are and hearing God's invitation to rest in his presence.

Perhaps the most spiritual thing we could do is get more rest so we are alert when we want to be alert. But we can also use our times of solitude as opportunities to rest in God. I have come to count on extended times of solitude as opportunities to take at least one nap, and I experience God's delight and care as I rest in him. There is a very deep kind of refreshment that comes when we incorporate rest into our times alone with God.

As I have paid more attention to my tiredness and fatigue, I have learned that there are at least two kinds of tired. One is what I call "good tired." This is the kind of tiredness we experience after a job well done, a task accomplished out of the best of who we are. If we are living in healthy rhythms of work and rest, this tiredness is a temporary condition, and when it comes, we know that after we take appropriate time for rest and recuperation, we will soon be back in the swing of things.

But another kind of tiredness is more ominous, and this is what I call "dangerous tired." It is deeper and more serious than the temporary exhaustion that follows periods of intensity of schedule and workload. The difference between "good tired" and "dangerous tired" is like the difference between the atmospheric conditions that produce harmless spring rain clouds and those that bring an eerie green-tinted sky and the possibility of a tornado. When the sky is green like that, you're not quite sure what's going on, but something doesn't feel right, and you know you had better pay attention. One atmospheric condition is normal and predictable; the other is risky and volatile.

Dangerous tired is an atmospheric condition of the soul that is volatile and portends the risk of great destruction. It is a chronic inner fatigue accumulating over months and months, and it does not always manifest itself in physical exhaustion. In fact, it can be masked by excessive activity and compulsive overworking. When we are dangerously tired we feel out of control, compelled to constant activity by inner impulses that we may not be aware of. For some reason we can't quite name, we're not able to linger and relax over a cup of coffee. We can't keep from checking voicemail or e-mail "just one more time" before we leave the office or before we go to bed at night. Or we can't stop cleaning or doing repairs and projects in order to take a walk in the evening or be quietly available to those we love. Rather than reading anything for the sheer pleasure of it, we pile the nightstand with books and professional journals that cram our heads full of information to keep us at "the top of our game." The idea of taking a full day off once a week seems impossible both in theory and in practice. We rarely, if ever, take a real break or vacation, choosing instead to work through holidays and break times. Not surprisingly, even when it is time for well-deserved sleep or rest, we may be unable to relax and receive this necessary gift.

While our way of life may seem heroic, there is a frenetic quality to our activity that is disturbing to those around us. When we do have discretionary time, we indulge in escapist behaviors—such as compulsive eating, drinking, spending, watching television—because we are too tired to choose activities that are truly life-giving.

When we are dangerously tired, we may be numb to the full range of human emotion. While it may seem like a relief to be unhampered by the negative emotions that bog other people down, in this condition the positive emotions become elusive as well. When we are dangerously tired we don't feel much of anything, good or bad. On some level we suspect that if we did stop long enough to experience our emotions, we might be overcome by feelings we'd rather not feel— sadness over past or present losses, desperation regarding aspects of our life or character that seem unfixable, powerlessness to choose the kind of life we know we're meant to live, unfulfilled desires and longings. We may be afraid that if we entered these unlit places in our souls, we might never come out.

One of the most sobering things I learned as I listened to my exhaustion and allowed God to minister to me is that when I am dangerously tired I can be very, very busy and look very, very important but be unable to hear the quiet, sure voice of the One who calls me the beloved. When that happens I lose touch with that place in the center of my being where I know who I am in God, where I know what I am called to do, and where I am responsive to his voice above all others. When that happens I am at the mercy of all manner of external forces, tossed and turned by others' expectations and my own compulsions. These inner lacks then become the source of my frenetic activity, keeping me forever spiraling into deeper levels of exhaustion.

As you read these words you may realize that you are teetering on the brink of dangerous tired—or that you are already over the edge. This can be a painful realization. But what would happen if, rather than judging and berating yourself, you lingered with your awareness, noticing the weariness that makes it hard for you to be attentive and alert in times of prayer and attentiveness to God? What would happen if you allowed yourself to wonder about your tiredness just a bit? Rather than criticizing yourself about falling asleep during prayer or your lack of interest in solitude, what if you gave yourself the freedom to notice your weariness *with compassion?* "Wow, I am really tired. I'm not sure I was aware of just how tired I am. What is that all about?"

Rather than distracting yourself in some way, what would happen if you chose to stay in God's presence and talk with him about your tiredness, acknowledging it as a child would with a parent who cares and can help? What if, rather than feeling alone and weighed down by the seeming impossibility of your situation, you invited God into it with a prayer: "Dear God, this tiredness is what's true about me. What are we going to do about it?"

Such honest noticing and questioning open up the opportunity for God to touch us and care for us in the midst of our humanness. In fact, the story of Elijah teaches us that if we do not rest ourselves, body, mind and soul, the journey into solitude and silence could very well be too much for us.

Practice
In silence, reflect on where you fall on the following continuum:

fully energized and refreshed	good tired	drifting toward dangerous tired	fully in a state of dangerous tired

As you identify where you are on the continuum, don't rush to try to solve or fix anything; instead, give yourself time and space to notice what is true about you. Invite God into this moment by saying, "God, this is what is true about me. What are we going to do about this?"

Allow yourself to become fully aware of God with you in these moments, loving you and extending compassion to you. Hear the words of Jesus spoken to you in these moments: "Come to me, all you that are weary and are carrying heavy burdens, and I will give you rest" (Mt 11:28). What is it like to hear these words right now? Do you believe it is possible for you to find the rest you need?

Tell God what you need, and listen for what he wants to say to you now.

5

Rest for the Body

I have calmed and quieted my soul,
   like a weaned child with its mother . . .

PSALM 131:2

No matter what state we're in, solitude gives us the opportunity to rest in God. The image of the satiated child resting against its mother is a picture of this rest, and that is good news for all of us who are more tired than we would like to be.

If we are basically rested and energized, solitude helps us maintain this healthy state, which is no small thing in a world that demands so much of us. If we are in a state of "good tired," solitude practiced regularly can prevent us from slipping unknowingly into a state of dangerous tired. If we have identified ourselves as being dangerously tired, solitude within the rhythms of daily life along with periodic extended times can help us find our way back to health.

But how exactly do we rest in God, given that God is not present with us physically and we feel far beyond the freedoms of infancy?

Learning to rest into God in times of solitude begins with the body, as the image of the nursing child suggests. This image takes me back to times that were both tender and tenuous in my life as a mother. When my oldest daughter, Charity, was born, I was barely twenty-two years old and felt a little overwhelmed by the weight of this responsibility. I wanted to give her what was best, and that seemed to include nursing. Although I hardly fit the earth-mother stereotype associated with the practice of nursing, I knew this choice would be good for me and for my baby, so that's what I did. And as I gave myself to the experience, I began to understand why.

Charity was a very intense child with little patience. She had her own ideas about where she wanted to be and was generally trying to squirm her way somewhere else when any of us held her. This was disappointing and frustrating at times when my whole self longed to cuddle and cradle this beautiful little girl. Nursing was the one time I could usually hold her and be with her in peace. Sometimes even the nursing was a struggle: no matter how hungry she was she would still sometimes resist settling down enough to take what was being offered. And when she did settle down she threw herself into the task of eating with a vengeance that was counterproductive.

Our best moments together were the moments immediately following nursing, when the need had been satisfied and the task was complete. Her body relaxed against mine in total peace and trust. Love was given and received at a deep experiential level through the intimacy of being heart to heart, skin to skin. Her gaze fastened on mine intensely; she was fully present with me, and we *experienced* each other at a level that was beyond words. What was most needed was given and received at the level where words are irrelevant. In that state of total relaxation Charity was able to enter into much-needed rest and I was able to be with her in a deeply satisfying way.

It is this kind of moment the psalmist is referring to in Psalm 131.

I believe God longs for these moments with us just as a mother anticipates the moments of peace, tranquility and communion that come after nursing her baby. Beyond the sheer enjoyment of it, God is much more aware than we are of how much we need "beyond words" togetherness. That is why he waits patiently for us to stop flailing around until we can relax and receive the nourishment of his presence.

We don't always think of caring for the body as a part of our spiritual practice, but the story of Elijah confirms that many times this is where it all begins. It can be hard and humbling to pay attention to your body, whatever state it is in, because it brings you face to face with your finiteness, your vulnerability. That in itself doesn't seem very relevant to the spiritual life. You may resist giving any kind of attention to the body because somewhere along the line you have learned to put the spiritual and the physical in separate compartments. You may believe that the spiritual journey takes place in a realm completely separate from the body. But the truth is that the spiritual journey is taken in a physical body, and there is a very real connection between caring for our body and deepening our relationship with God.

What a surprise it has been to find that, in the mist of my spiritual journey, I have been forced to face my profound ambivalence about life in a body. Intent on trying to live up to a misguided spiritual ideal, I had relegated life in the body to some lesser category that warranted very little of my attention. As long as my body wasn't causing me any overwhelming problems, I could ignore it in favor of obviously spiritual endeavors such as Scripture reflection, prayer and service to others. Rather than caring for my body and valuing it as I would any other highly valued gift, I mostly ignored it, assuming it had nothing to do with life in the Spirit.

At first giving attention to my body in the context of solitude and silence felt uncomfortable and embarrassing, and I resisted it mightily. I resisted not only because it didn't seem very spiritual (and I was into feeling spiritual) but also because I didn't like what I saw. In addition to the more obvious symptoms of exhaustion, I started to become aware of the way I carried tension in my shoulders, the way I "forgot" to breathe when I was nervous or unsure or uptight, the way the cares and concerns of the day kept me awake at night because I don't know how to rest in God, the way certain activities energized me and others left me inordinately drained. I wasn't sure what to do with what I was noticing.

This is how one woman describes what she noticed in her body during initial experiences with silence:

> Breathing, stretching and silence are *all* hard for me. I feel physically wound up, full of kinks. My heart beats too fast and my breathing is shallow. To try and breathe deeply makes me very uncomfortable, almost panicky—a feeling I remember having even as a child. I am definitely hyped up by caffeine, and trying to do this meditation is showing me that, and showing me that my body is really crying out for a new kind of peace and restedness. It's as if I've been on an adrenalin high my whole life! . . . I'm so wound-up and tired and full of knots and tension.

It is not unusual to experience such uncomfortable awareness. But despite the discomfort we might feel about giving our bodies careful attention, in solitude we learn to listen to our body's need for rest and relief from the tension it carries. The more we are willing to listen to our physical condition and respond with greater care, the more we discover that the physical and the spiritual are not as disconnected as we had assumed.

As I shifted my living patterns in response to what I was noticing, some significant changes began to take place. I began getting more true rest (rather than resorting to the short-lived benefits of caffeine), eating nutritious food, drinking more water, paying attention to my breathing and working my way slowly into a more active lifestyle. I began to feel more energetic and alert in all activities, including the time I spent in solitude. Rather than showing up tired and distracted, I began to bring a self that was alert, energized and ready to respond to the Lover of my soul.

One of God's gifts to us is that physical exercise releases endorphins that can soothe our emotions, ease pain and elevate our mood. Because I can get lost in fits of morbid introspection and spiraling subjectivity, I realized that I needed these lifts to my spirit; they were God's gifts for my soul through the medium of my body. I even began to expand my definition of solitude. To be in solitude it is not necessary to sit quietly! In fact, slow, meditative walks, jogs and bike rides have become very important parts of my practice of solitude. It seems that while my body is on automatic pilot and enjoying the release that comes with physical activity, my mind and soul are less distracted and can be more fully present to God. Partic-

> The Christian practice of honoring the body is born in the confidence that our bodies are made in the image of God's own goodness. . . . As the place where the divine Presence dwells, our bodies are worthy of care and blessing and ought never to be degraded or exploited. It is through our bodies that we participate in God's activity in the world.
>
> DOROTHY BASS, *PRACTICING OUR FAITH*

ularly when I walk or jog at the end of the day, I do so in conscious awareness of being with God. Together we reflect on the events of the day from beginning to end, and I invite God to reveal evidences of his presence with me, clues I may have missed in the rush of things. This creates time and space for wonder and gratitude at the ways the Divine intersects with the human in the midst of the ordinariness of my life. It gives opportunity for gratitude to become a powerful source of energy for my spiritual life.

I also invite God to show me those times I may not have been as loving as I want to be or times I may have failed to notice or respond to a prompting of the Holy Spirit. If I need to confess sin or learn from a mistake, I do that as God and I take our evening walk together. The practice of reviewing my day with God is rooted in the ancient Christian practices of *examen of consciousness* (looking back over the day to notice God's presence) and *examen of conscience* (noticing my response or lack of response to that presence). It helps me to release the events of this day to God, which then enables me to receive the gift of sleep that night and live in the new mercies that are awaiting me when I wake up the next morning.

In all of these ways and more I have begun to embrace the truth that I am not merely a soul and spirit; I am an *embodied* human being, and this body is the dwelling place of the Holy Spirit. It is a temple, a place set apart for meeting with God. In some inexplicable way God inhabits our bodies, making them a place where we can meet and know him (1 Cor 6:19).

In the quiet listening and noticing that solitude affords, I am able to monitor the ways I allow this temple to become a bit run down so it is not quite up to the rigors of meeting with the living God. When I am able to open up to that reality in God's presence, it becomes an opportunity to work together with God on fashioning a life where the needs of the body are cared for as a part of my commitment to the spiritual journey.

When I'm able to get away for a longer retreat of solitude (twenty-four hours or more), I have learned to begin with a good night's sleep. If I am on retreat just for a day, I usually start with a nap. For a long time I tried to arrive at my retreats well rested, but that proved to be impossible for me—and most people I know. Usually it is all I can do to just get there; in fact, it often takes a lot of *extra* effort and energy to clear time for a personal retreat. So I have come to accept that I will arrive a bit tired. I no longer feel guilty about incorporating rest into my retreat times, because "[God] gives sleep to his beloved" (Ps 127:2). Time and space to rest the body is a gift God gave Elijah, and it is a gift he wants to give us as well.

Learning to listen to the body, to rest it and honor it as a place where God makes his presence known, becomes, then, an important discipline for the spiritual pilgrim.

Practice

Take three deep, slow breaths—long inhalations as well as exhalations. Close your eyes if that helps you to relax into your breathing. Let your intent be to rest your whole self into God, knowing you are as safe with him as a baby is with his mother.

As you breathe, notice what happens in your body. Where are the tight places that relax as you breathe? Is there any way your body wants to shift or change position in order to be more comfortable? Make whatever adjustments will deepen your rest.

Continue to breathe, resting openly and simply in God's presence for a few moments. Notice how things are with your body these days. What feels tired? What feels energized? What hurts or aches or feels tight? What feels good and strong and well? Does your body feel loved and cared for or unbalanced and abused?

Is there anything God seems to want to give you right now in response to your body's need: a few minutes to curl up and rest under a warm blanket, a quiet walk, time to just keep sitting and relishing his presence?

Allow yourself to rest in God in this physical, tangible way for as long as you can in your time of solitude. Close your silence with a brief prayer of gratitude for God's care experienced in these moments. Ask him to help you to remain in this resting stance in whatever activity you enter next.

6

Rest for the Mind

> My heart is not lifted up,
>> my eyes are not raised too high;
> I do not occupy myself with things
>> too great and too marvelous for me.

PSALM 131:1

Once we've gotten accustomed to resting the body and paying attention to it in times of solitude, we are faced with an even more formidable challenge: resting the mind. The psalmist's description of the mind at rest in God is powerful both in its simplicity and in its seeming impossibility for the modern mind. The truth about me is that I seem to *always* be occupying myself with things too great and too marvelous for me—that is, things too complicated and weighty for the human mind to comprehend or figure out. Yesterday I wanted to fix my marriage, today I want to fix my children, tomorrow I'll try to fix the world. It's always something.

The human mind is perpetually busy trying to control things, trying to figure things out, clinging to the latest idea, grasping at the nearest straw. It works very hard trying to make sense of things by endlessly seeking to put everything into categories and boxes and systems of thought. Sometimes even God himself gets relegated to a category or a box *in my mind* rather than being free to be God *in my life*. It seems that my mind will go to great lengths to fix things, control things and defend against anything that would disrupt my carefully constructed equilibrium.

One of my most startling realizations about the unceasing nature of my mind's work came the first time my husband told me that during the night I had sat up in bed and launched into the introduction to a new message. What surprised him the most was that this sleepy sermon was coherent and came out in complete sentences. He said his only regret was that he hadn't taken notes. I wished he had taken notes too because then I would have had my introduction. We have laughed often about this idiosyncrasy, but in this strange way I have discovered that even when we are able to get our body to rest, it can be a more daunting task to quiet and rest the mind.

In solitude I make the frustrating discovery that often my mind keeps me flailing around rather than settling into rest in God. I begin to notice all the ways my mind distracts me from the very thing my soul is longing for, the experience of rest, union and communion with God. Oh, how our minds need to learn how to rest in the way the psalmist describes!

It's not that the mind is bad; it's just very limited in its capacity to move us toward the union with God that we seek. The intellect can set the stage but cannot provide the drama of true encounter. Our experience with human relationships tells us this: thinking about someone is not the same thing as being in their presence. Knowing facts about someone, studying the details of their life, admiring them from afar is not the same as being in relationship with them or allowing oneself to fall in love. Jesus underscores the point when he tells us to love God and that the place where the drama of loving encounter takes place is not first and foremost the mind. It is the heart and soul: "You shall love the Lord your God with all your heart, and with all your soul, and with all your mind" (Mt 22:37, quoting Deut 6:5).

If we are able to notice the difference between what goes on in the mind and what goes on in the heart, we might eventually acknowledge that our mind is tired of trying to hold it all together, figure everything out, make something happen. We might notice the ways our wordy prayers keep us working at things in our head rather than allowing our mind to rest in God's heart of love, where his good intentions toward us can make themselves known.

If we are able to stay with our frustrations long enough and not give up, we may begin to suspect that the things that most need to be known and solved and figured out in our life are not going to be discovered, solved or figured out at the thinking level anyway. The things we most need to know, solve and figure out will be *heard* at

How can we possibly expect anyone to find real nurture, comfort, and consolation from a prayer life that takes the mind beyond its limits and adds one more exhausting activity to the many already scheduled ones? . . . Often it seems that we find ourselves entangled in such a complex network of discussions, debates, and arguments about God and "God-issues" that a simple conversation with God or a simple presence to God have become practically impossible.

HENRI NOUWEN, THE WAY OF THE HEART

the listening level, that place within us where God's Spirit witnesses with our spirit (Rom 8:16). Here God speaks to us of things that cannot be understood through human wisdom or shuffled around and filed away in the mind (1 Cor 2:10-13). Spiritual discernment is given as pure gift in God's way, in God's time, beyond what the human mind can force (1 Cor 2:14). At this level we find ourselves loved to the extent that fear is cast out so we are free to hear and respond to the risky invitations of God. To hear at this level we must rest from our striving. We must let go of everything our mind is holding on to in order to receive the revelation that comes from beyond ourselves.

I am sure one of the reasons my own spiritual director let me talk for so long in the early stages of my spiritual direction was so I would *experience* the limitations of my mind. I needed to experience the fact that my mental sorting and calculating and my efforts to process everything with words were not getting me anywhere. This was a hard reality to face, and I railed against it. I still do sometimes. Accepting the limitations of the mind flies in the face of everything my cultural and religious background has taught me about how we come to know things. I'm not sure I can trust anything but my mind.

But what happens when we hit the wall of mental impasse? What happens when no amount of hard mental work gives us what we need—answers, guidance, love, transformation of some intractable pattern? What happens then? Well, we squirm for a while, pinned to the wall by the nail of this truth: our poverty, our impotence, our need for something beyond what the human mind can generate.

That's the bad news.

The good news is that finally, when we are exhausted from squirming, we may open up to the possibility of letting go of our own efforts and receiving something from God. If we give in to our exhaustion in this way and stop flailing around, we may become willing to stop the flow of our own words and listen for a while. Silence is the practice that allows us to do this. Psalm 46:10 tells us there is a kind of knowing that comes in silence and not in words—but first we must be still.

The Hebrew word translated "Be still" literally means "Let go of your grip." Let go of your grip on your own understanding. Cease striving at the level of human effort, and in so doing open yourself to a whole new kind of knowing.

It is not that we seek to ignore the intellect (or any other aspect of ourselves for that matter) in times of solitude; instead we let the mind settle into the heart, the very center of our being where God dwells in us as redeemed people.

We often think of the heart as the seat of our emotional life, the place where we feel and express sentiment. However, the word *heart* in biblical and spiritual tradition is much richer than that. In Jewish-Christian tradition the heart encompasses the very essence of who we are, the core of our moral nature and our spiritual life. From the heart flow all of our physical, emotional, intellectual, volitional and moral energies; it is the very spring of our life (Prov 4:23). The heart is the sphere of divine influence, or it is the arena of divine-human interaction.

Silence helps us drop beneath the superficiality of our mental constructs to that place of the heart that is deeper in its reality than anything the mind can capture or express in words. It is a place of longing and desire and reaching for that which we do not yet have. In this wordless place the whole of our person turns itself toward God and waits to be addressed by God. This kind of prayer is

> standing in the presence of God with the mind in the heart; that is, at the point of our being where there are no divisions or distinctions and where we are totally one. There God's spirit dwells and there the great encounter takes place. There heart speaks to heart, because there we stand before the face of the Lord, all-seeing within us.

In silence we begin to recognize that a lot of our God-talk is like the finger that points to the moon. The finger that points to the moon is not the moon. Pointing to the moon, talking about the moon, involving ourselves in study and explanation about how the light of the moon is generated is not the same thing as sitting in moonlight, letting moonbeams fall around us illuminating what they will. It is not the same thing as noticing how everything is transformed in this numinous light. When we sit in the light of the moon, we don't try to figure it out, explain it or force it to be anything other than what it is. We just enjoy sitting in the midst of it.

It is the same with God. Our words *about* God are not the Reality itself. They are only the finger pointing to the moon. In silence we give in to the fact that our words can never contain God or adequately describe our experiences with God. When we give in to the exhaustion that comes from trying to put everything into words and mental concepts, we give our mind permission to just stop. We give ourselves over to the *experience* of the Reality itself.

In the crucible of silence, the wall of mental impasse ceases to be the place where we are skewered by our human impotence and instead becomes the very breast of God. Eventually there is a strength born of quietness and confidence, because time and time again we have found there everything we need for our sustenance. This is a very deep kind of rest indeed.

> *Be patient toward all that is unsolved in your heart and try to love the questions themselves like locked rooms and like books that are written in a very foreign tongue. Do not seek the answers, which cannot be given you because you would not be able to live them. And the point is to live everything. Live the questions now. Perhaps you will then gradually, without noticing it, live along some distant day into the answer.*
>
> RAINER MARIE RILKE, *LETTERS TO A YOUNG POET*

Practice

Take three long, deep breaths to help yourself settle into the silence. Notice how the breathing helps you release any physical tension that might be distracting you. Notice (if you can) the different levels of your being, particularly the difference between your mind and your heart. Give yourself a few moments to notice and experience what is going on in your mind and what is going on in your heart.

What is it you need to know in the stillness that you haven't been able to know in the noisiness and busyness of your mind? What is the "I don't know" place in your life that no amount of thinking and wordiness has been able to touch with any kind of answer?

Sit with God with your question. Say it out loud. Tell him how it feels not to have the answer, but resist the urge to grasp for answers, to force clarity that isn't there or cling to mental processes for figuring things out. Allow related issues, concerns and thoughts to present themselves, but don't dwell on them. Let them pass by like clouds in the sky. Rather than trying to figure anything out or grasp for anything, rest in God's presence with your question.

If you notice yourself becoming impatient, ask, *Am I willing to be patient with this thing that is unsolved in my heart? What would it look like for me to stop working so hard on this and trust God to work in his way and his time?*

Sit in silence for as long a time as you have allotted. Close your time of silence by praying the Lord's Prayer, allowing the words and phrases to shape your response to your question and to the next activity you engage in.

7

Rest for the Soul

Truly I tell you, unless you change and become like children, you will never enter the kingdom of heaven.

JESUS

We all need a place to be a child, no matter how old we are. Young children who have been well cared for seem to have an instinctual trust in the unconditional acceptance of those who love them, and so they are able to let down and relax when they need to. They don't yet know how to put on airs. They don't try to make things look better than they are. They haven't yet learned how to hold back their squeals of delight, their expressions of need or desire, their tears of sadness or pain. Children seem to be uninhibited about expressing whatever is true of them in the present moment. Sometimes it's cute and adorable; often it is less so. But part of being a child is being re-laxed and at home with yourself, with the people around you, with life itself.

And so it is with the soul at rest in God. We do not put on airs. We do not try to make things seem better than they are. We do not pretend to be someone or something we are not. We do not hold back squeals of delight, expressions of need or desire, tears of pain, sadness or disappointment. In times of solitude, the soul rests in God by simply *being with God with what is.*

In a way this is a bit like the game Musical Chairs: while the music of life plays you go around and around and around, but when the music stops you sit down right where you are, and that's where you are—sweaty, out of breath, heart pounding, perhaps triumphant (if you made it through one more round) or a little disappointed (if you've been sidelined). But wherever you are is where you are.

When we stop the music of our life to enter into solitude, we sit down right where we are at that moment, and that's where we meet God. We meet God in our present delight or our present sadness. We meet God in the tears of our life and the laughter of our life. We meet God in our most unnerving questions and in the answers we are celebrating. No matter where we are on any given day, when the music stops and everything gets quiet, we sit down right where we are and allow ourselves to be there with him.

How desperately our souls need regular moments like that, moments when we rest in God and allow ourselves to be with God with what is most true about us. Early on in my attempts at solitude, I wasted a lot of energy trying to get myself "all prettied up" so I could be a certain way for God. I tried to get all of my relationships into good shape, all of my sins confessed, all of my major issues solved. I tried to make sure all of my voicemails had been answered and my inbox was empty; heck, I even tried to make sure the dishes were done and the bathroom floor was clean before entering into solitude—as if God really cared about that! I didn't want to leave *anything* undone or unsanitary in my life that might distract me or God from all the spiritual things we were supposed to be about.

All this pressure made solitude seem quite overwhelming and exhausting. If my soul did rest at all, it was only because I was practically comatose from working so hard to get ready! After repeatedly failing to sanitize my life to my own satisfaction, I suspected I was missing the point. The point of solitude is to be with God with what is true about me right now—whatever that is. Silence, then, allows me to simply give God access to the reality of myself. With the same trust and lack of inhibition that a child demonstrates with her mother, I can rest against God and allow him to care for my soul as only he can.

Some days when the music stops and we sit down right where we are, we get to be with God in pleasant places—perhaps in the midst of gratitude. Not too long ago I was on a flight from Chicago to Kansas City late one Friday night. I was actually in the middle of a speaking engagement that had been scheduled far in advance and ended up coinciding with my daughter's senior prom. Through the understanding and flexibility of the sponsoring organization and a few of my colleagues, I had been able to fly back to Chicago in the middle of the teaching assignment so I could help Charity get dressed and be with her for her pictures. Then I hopped back on a plane so I could teach all day Saturday in Kansas City.

When I collapsed onto my seat that Friday night, the cabin was nearly empty. It was dark and quiet in a comforting way, and I found myself with about an hour and fifteen minutes of unexpected solitude. Even though I had books and papers with me, I felt drawn to just be with God, bringing my gratitude for being able to be with my daughter at an important moment of her life, a moment in which only a mom would do. I remembered the graciousness of the person responsible for engaging the event speakers: she said, "In the whole scheme of things, no one is going to remember this conference, but your daughter will always remember whether or not you were at her senior prom." How relieved I had been to receive such kindness and understanding! I reflected with gratitude on each person who had had helped me there and back. I thought of the flights and ground transportation and traffic patterns that were on time and free of problems. I lingered over the beauty of the moments with Charity and allowed my heart to stir with the joy and pride of a mother who sees her daughter so beautiful and grown up.

And I was grateful.

It wasn't the first time I had ever felt gratitude; but it was the first time I had ever given it that much space. Instead of rushing on to the next thing, I let thanksgiving fill every corner of my soul. I felt it and relished it down to the tips of my toes.

Those moments were absolutely delicious, and I was so glad I had not reflexively reached for "stuff" to distract me rather sitting with God with what was true about me in that moment. But later I noticed something else. As the weekend continued, I realized that the benefits of giving time and space for gratitude went far beyond the moment. The experience of gratitude, spread through my soul in solitude, became a source of powerful energy for my ministry the next day and for the events of the next week. Naturally I was tired after the speaking engagement, but I was not exhausted. Creating space for gratitude rather than letting it slip by unnoticed became deeply replenishing in a way that mere sleep could not have accomplished.

The other side of the coin, of course, is that some days when the music stops we need to be with God with more difficult realities: grief, fear, pain, confusion. Recently I had to grieve a deeply personal loss, one I was unable to adequately express to anyone. During my early morning time in solitude, I acknowledged it to God by writing about it in my journal. I told God how angry I was about this loss—and recognized my fear that this anger might be completely debilitating if I really let myself feel it. Because I wasn't sure I would be able to pull myself back together and function if I allowed myself to fully experience my grief, I chose not go any further than acknowledging my feelings at that point. I knew that the work of grieving would have to be done eventually, but I wasn't ready, so I got busy with my day.

I held it all together for a productive morning, but by lunchtime the sadness and despair were pressing in. I knew I needed to open some space to be with God with what was true about me. I needed to give in to the fact that I did not have a clue about what to do with and for myself. I needed to give in to the magnitude of the loss and accompanying emotion, without knowing how it would be comforted or what the outcomes would be. Everything in me screamed for a distraction, but for a little while at least, I needed to refuse to distract myself with achievement, busyness, noise or human interaction. I needed to open my grief to God and see what he would do in that place. So I decided to open myself to the possibility of true comfort, as risky as it seemed.

What deadens us most to God's presence within, I think, is the inner dialogue that we are engaged in within ourselves, the endless chatter of human thought. I suspect that there is nothing more crucial to true spiritual comfort than being able from time to time to stop that chatter, including the chatter of spoken prayer.

FREDERICK BUECHNER, *TELLING SECRETS*

All I could think to do was to crawl back into bed, knowing that I was in God's presence and it was good to come to God with my grief, just as it is good for a child to come to a mother or father with his grief. On this day, solitude and silence meant allowing the waves of pain to wash over me (even though I was afraid I might be swept away) and allowing the tears to come (even though I really do hate to cry).

And the waves of pain did wash over me with a rhythmic quality. Ebbing and flowing. Coming and going. I felt I needed to lie completely still so as not to be swept away. At times I came close to falling asleep, and I wanted to. I wished desperately for some kind of escape from what I was feeling, but God kept me awake. There was no escape, no way out except to go all the way through it.

In time—a couple hours I think—the waves of grief subsided.

It is hard to describe what happened after that: I find it inexplicable the way God comes to us and ministers to us when we are willing to trust ourselves to him. God's way of making his presence known and comforting us in such moments is as individualized and personal as each mother's way of holding and comforting her own child; it is a very intimate thing. Going all the way into the grief in God's presence left me feeling tender and vulnerable, but I could also sense that I was held safely. I felt empty and spent, but I also felt comforted by God's loving presence. I knew I was not alone in my grief. Nothing was fixed, but I was okay. I had not been swept away.

The next morning the prayer from the devotional guide I use for private worship contained these words.

Lord of life and love . . . quiet our souls in thy presence with the stillness of a wise trust.
[So that's what the stillness of yesterday was about!]

Lift us above dark moods, and the shadow of sin,
[I need you to lift me above this grief rather than being tempted to run from its reality.]

That we may find thy will for our lives;
*[Yes, God, one thing I am sure of is that I still want to know and do
your will even in the midst of this grief.]*

Through Jesus Christ our Lord.
*[I know that there is no other way this grief will be comforted except
through Christ.]*

Amen.

Practice

Some days you can easily be with God with both gratitude and grief. At
other times one or the other is predominant, and you need to go with
what is most pressing. The following exercise is well suited to become
a regular part of your extended solitude times as a way of resting in God.

Quiet yourself in God's presence by taking several deep breaths. As
you silence the music of your life, is there anything that is hurting
these days, any grief you have been holding in? It need not be anything momentous; it could be something that feels relatively insignif-
icant such as a hurtful interaction with someone who matters to you,
or being left out of something you wanted to be included in. Allow
whatever is weighing on your soul right now to come to the surface—whether it seems big or small.

Let yourself experience the grief, but do so with the awareness that
you are not alone. You are in the presence of the One who loves you
and bears your grief with you. Notice whether your body wants to
express the grief through kneeling, lying flat on the floor, shedding
tears or sitting in utter stillness, and allow that to happen. You may
want to use these words as your prayer: "In silence my soul waits for
you alone, O God; from you alone comes my salvation" (a personal-
ization of Ps 62:1).

Is there something you are feeling especially grateful for these days? Where are you experiencing life and authentic connection with God and others?

Allow time to just experience your gratitude in God's presence. Don't feel you have to *do* anything except to bask in the goodness of God toward you. If you want to say anything to God or journal your thoughts, feel free to do so, but don't feel that you have to.

8

Emptiness

Inner silence depends on a continual seeking, a continual
crying in the night, a repeated bending over the abyss. . . .
For He is found when He is sought, and when He is
no longer sought, He escapes us.

THOMAS MERTON

The invitation to solitude and silence does not end with us sitting
under a solitary broom tree eating angel-food cakes. The strengthen-
ing of body and soul is prerequisite for a journey ahead, a pilgrimage
that leads into the empty places of the wilderness.

When the angel of God rouses Elijah from his sleep the second
time to offer him food and drink, he says, "Get up and eat, otherwise
the journey will be too much for you."

I imagine Elijah sputtering, "What journey? I thought I made myself pretty clear. I said I was done. Finished. I'm kind of enjoying this
little picnic under the solitary broom tree, and I'm not going anywhere!" That is certainly how I have responded at times to the deeper
invitations of the spiritual life.

Just when it seems I am getting pieced back together, I start receiving the message that this rest, this guidance for the renewal of body and soul, has been only a beginning: there is a journey ahead, and it is not just any journey. It is actually a quest that will be rather demanding, requiring all the strength and stamina I have gained in rest. In fact, I have a sneaking suspicion that everything I've gone through so far is just preparation! No matter that I thought I made myself clear that I am finished, I am empty, I have nothing left. God has a different read on the whole situation. He says, "Great! You have now finally left behind all the external trappings that just get in the way on the spiritual journey. You are starting to become empty enough— empty of your reliance on yourself and empty of those things that satisfy only briefly—to begin hungering for a more substantive experience of my presence."

Fortunately, if we have done our resting, things are starting to shift so we are getting clearer about what we want. In Elijah's resting, he gained clarity and resolve that had been impossible for him to find when he was desperately tired. This is true for all of us. Once we get a little rest, we start to get our perspective back. Rather than reacting to everything around us, we start to have a sense of what is truly called for in our life.

For Elijah, it became clear that he wanted and needed an encounter with God. In fact, he became willing to leave everything else behind in order to find that. He was willing to walk away—at least temporarily— from his intimate relationships, his past successes, his prominence as a prophet in Israel, the forms and rituals and places of worship to which he was accustomed, and any kind of physical and emotional security. He was willing to leave all this behind for *the mere possibility* of finding God in some way that would heal the disillusionment of his life. Prophets, of all people, know visitations from God are never guaranteed.

So, after fortifying himself one more time with food and drink, Elijah got up and started his journey to Mt. Horeb, also known as Mt. Sinai. Why Mt. Horeb? Because deep in Elijah's history, deep in his spiritual experience, he was aware that this was a place of possibility: this was the place where the people of Israel encountered God when they needed God most. Here God had called to Moses from the burning bush. Later on, when Moses desperately needed to know that God would go with him to the Promised Land, this mountain was where God himself passed by and assured Moses that his presence would go with him wherever he went. This was where God gave Moses the Ten Commandments and established his covenant with his chosen people. If there was any place on the planet where one might go in hopes of encountering God, Mt. Horeb was it.

Elijah was hungry for an experience of divine Presence, and even the public display of God's power in the fire that consumed the altars of Baal could not fully satisfy that hunger. He had some inkling of where to go to find what he was looking for, and he was willing to walk faithfully and resolutely in that direction.

On top of this willingness to walk *away from* the peopled places of his life, places that had a bit of definition, Elijah had an even deeper willingness: he was willing to walk *into* the emptiness of the wilderness in order to find what he was looking for. As I write I have my Bible open to a map of the Holy Land, and I notice for the first time that Mt. Horeb is surrounded by desert—and not just one desert but five or six! The desert of Sinai, the desert of Zin, the desert of Shur, the desert of Paran, the Eastern Desert . . . The vastness of the empty spaces around this sacred place where God visited his people takes my breath away.

Elijah walked through the emptiness of the desert for *forty days and forty nights* until he settled into a cave on the side of Mt. Horeb, and there he waited for a visitation from God. He probably had no idea when, if or how anything even remotely meaningful would happen, but he was willing to stay in the emptiness until it did.

Elijah's wilderness experience is a powerful metaphor for the vast emptiness all of us must walk through on the way to encounter with God. But how we as human beings seek to avoid this truth of the spiritual life! The experience of our emptiness is so painful we will do almost anything to avoid it—and most of us do for a long, long time. But try as we might, we cannot escape the fact that willingness to walk into the empty places is a precursor to finding God—in Elijah's life and in our own. As Dan Allender writes in *The Healing Path*,

> Our spiritual journey must lead through the desert or else our healing will be the product of our own will and wisdom. It is in the silence of the desert that we hear our dependence on noise. It is in the poverty of the desert that we see clearly our attachments to the trinkets and baubles we cling to for security and pleasure. The desert shatters the soul's arrogance and leaves body and soul crying out in thirst and hunger. In the desert we trust God or die.

If the truth be told, I could chronicle my entire spiritual journey by tracking my experiences of emptiness and how these experiences— painful as they are—open me the substance of God. One of my earliest experiences with emptiness came as a skinny, awkward teenage girl with glasses and braces, volatile skin, and clothes that had been handed down to me as "the pastor's kid." The emptiness and longing I experienced as I watched the "beautiful ones" with their perfect skin and teeth, perky breasts, and cheerleading outfits (symbols of belonging and acceptance) seemed unfathomable. The only thing that even remotely touched this longing was being able to journal my thoughts and prayers and disappointments to God. Maybe I thought if I could name it I could fix it. Maybe writing to Someone gave me a way to live into my belief that God existed in the midst of my emptiness. Or maybe the words on the page helped me to believe *I* existed even though I was all but invisible to my high school classmates. All I knew then was that, in those moments, turning my whole self to God by journaling helped me.

Now I know that my high school experience of emptiness—and the choice not to numb that emptiness in the ways teenagers often do—forced me to cling to God with the desperation of one hanging over an abyss. It enlarged my capacity for God and enabled me to receive the presence of God. This would have been totally unnecessary if my life had been full of all I thought I wanted.

Of course, my experiences with emptiness did not end there. They continue to this day. As recently as last week I pulled away for a day of solitude on fairly short notice because I was aware of becoming demanding and impatient in a couple of my relationships, my pace of activity was approaching the frenetic level, and I struggled with anxiety and lack of acceptance of the limitations of my life. Something was not quite right. As I approached the hermitage where I would spend this day in solitude, I recognized once again the familiar yawning emptiness and longing underneath the surface of my life. Because I hadn't opened it to God for a while, I had been trying to assuage the emptiness in all my old ways. It hadn't yet gotten to the point where it was obvious to the whole world (thank God!), but it was obvious to me and to those closest to me, and I needed to pay attention.

You would think all these years later it would be easy to walk into the emptiness, but it still gives me pause. On this day, everything in me wanted to do something else—go shopping, read a novel, write another chapter *about* solitude rather than actually giving into the demands of solitude. Even doing dishes and folding laundry seemed like an attractive option!

But refusing to walk into the emptiness does no good over the long haul. The abyss of emptiness will only widen until it starts devouring the things we value most with its insatiable hunger. We, like Elijah, must walk across the emptiness of the desert "out there" to arrive at the mouth of the cave that is the emptiness "in here." But this is a brave thing to do. Most of us spend our whole life trying to avoid the experience of being empty and alone. True solitude allows none of the usual escapes.

On this day I became aware of at least three deserts that need to be crossed in my own life—there was an empty place in my marriage I grieved, there was an unresolved relationship I could not fix, and I had had a painful physical injury that prevented me from being active in the ways that are life-giving to me. It took me awhile to even acknowledge these empty places with God. I didn't really want to walk into them, because I knew that fixing was not on the agenda for this day, and there was nothing to distract me from such unpleasantness.

About halfway through the day I was ready to walk into it all. First I was angry, and that scared me because I am not very nice when I am angry. But I decided God could take it and I told him anyway. Under the anger was sadness, which I don't like very much either. Sadness seems like such a weak and useless emotion compared to anger, which at least gives me some energy to do something about the problem! Sadness feels like a deep pit with dark water at the bottom that threatens to overwhelm me before I can find my way out.

But one way God visited me on this day was that he helped me to cry, which I don't do often enough. And as much as I was afraid of being drowned by my emotion, I found that the tears were a gift: they softened me, they helped me to let go and breathe, they caused me to open rather than continuing to hold myself so tight and defended against realities I didn't want to face. I was unaware of how hard and closed I had become.

After the tears things were clearer, like blue skies after the dark clouds have emptied themselves of rain. I found I was cleared out of my anxious striving, cleared out of my anger, no longer afraid of the sadness. After the tears I was empty, but it was a different kind of emptiness. Rather than the kind of emptiness that causes me to clutch and grasp at the nearest fix, this emptiness made me soft and open like a hand outstretched and ready to receive. Receive what? I didn't know. I stayed in that emptiness until it was time to go home.

As I left my time in solitude, it didn't seem as if much had happened, which was a bit disconcerting. But as I reenter life in the company of others, I realize that something has shifted inside. Although I'm not quite sure when or how, I notice that I am no longer resisting the emptiness. Now that God and I have gone there together, it is not as scary as it used to be. I recognize the empty place in my marriage as a part of the reality Rainer Maria Rilke refers to when he writes, "True love consists in this, that two solitudes protect and border and salute each other." At least for this day I accept the fact that even marriage cannot insulate me from the pain of separateness that is part of the human experience. I am able to embrace the reality that this experience is a good thing—ultimately—because it keeps my heart turned toward God.

I no longer fight against the pain of the unresolved relationship; instead I experience the pain without trying to fix it. I am glad that I still care enough to feel the pain; it means I am alive in the ways I want to be alive. It causes me to pray. At least for this day, I accept this lack of resolution as part of the unfinished work of our lives, while knowing that what is unfinished has already been finished at the cosmic level in Christ.

I face the fears, concerns and frustrations I feel about my injured ankle. The frustration and sadness I feel about not being able to walk or run or bike today is all I can handle, so I set a boundary on my heart. I agree with God not to jump ahead to the potential worries of tomorrow: Will my ankle heal all the way? Will I ever be able to run and bike again? How do I live without the physical activities I have come to enjoy so much? Tomorrow will have to take care of itself.

The gift of solitude on this day is that I was able to walk into my emptiness and I didn't get lost in it. And I think that is what I am most afraid of—that I will get lost in the emptiness and stay in the wilderness forever. But that is not what happens. Instead, an imperceptible filling—hardly even noticeable—is taking place in my soul. While the experience of being empty is painful, emptiness is prerequisite to being filled. As it turns out, the presence of God is poured out most generously when there is space in our souls to receive him. In the vast emptiness of the human soul there is finally room for God.

Practice

All of us have places in our life that feel very empty; sometimes they exist simultaneously with places that are very full. The empty places are the ones we usually try to avoid, yet God is waiting to meet us in the midst of our emptiness. Where are the empty places in your life right now? Are you willing to acknowledge them and walk into them as Elijah did?

During your time in silence, sit with your hands gently open on your lap as a way of expressing your willingness to be empty in God's presence. Sit in the place of emptiness in your life, and imagine that it is a receptacle for the very presence of God. Remember that we cannot demand that God fill the emptiness on our terms. Let it be enough to experience your emptiness in a new way—no longer as a scary, dark and barren place but as a place of openness, receptivity and spiritual possibility.

9

Facing Ourselves

Solitude is the furnace of transformation. . . . [It] is the place of the great struggle and the great encounter—the struggle against the compulsions of the false self, and the encounter with the loving God who offers himself as the substance of the new self.

HENRI NOUWEN

If Elijah's story tells us anything, it tells us that solitude and silence offer no quick fixes. Elijah walked in the outer emptiness of the desert for forty days and forty nights, and God still had not made himself known. As Elijah settled into the cave of his inner emptiness, God had not done anything very Godlike, and all Elijah could do was wait through the darkness of the night.

This is the part of Elijah's story I am tempted to sidestep, because I, for one, do not like to wait. In the grocery store, in the doctor's office, at the hair salon—if there is even a few minutes' wait, everything in me rises up in churning rebellion against this nonproductive use of time. My frustration intensifies when I realize that I am caught: caught between my need for what I am waiting for and my impatience with the waiting. Yes, I could leave my cart and walk out of the grocery store, but then I am still without the groceries I need. I could walk out of the doctor's office in a huff because the wait is too long, but I am still left with my need for medical attention. I could leave the hair salon insulted that the world has not arranged itself for my convenience, but I'm still going to need a haircut.

Waiting, in the realm of the soul, presents us with the same agony. We sit in the waiting room of the soul because we need something. Yes, we could get up and leave, but we would be walking away from the very place where our need could be met. And so we remain in the waiting place, totally at the mercy of God's timing and initiative in our life.

And sooner or later God does make himself known. In Elijah's case he shows up with a question. On the surface it appears to be a simple question, but when it is God doing the asking somehow the question is sharply penetrating.

"What are you doing here, Elijah?"

It's a good question, a question I have often asked myself in solitude. What am I doing here? What am I *doing?* Who am I when I'm not doing? Won't the world just pass me by while I'm sitting here doing nothing?

How easy it would be to fudge on the true reason for being in this waiting room of the soul: *I needed a little vacation. Needed a change of scenery. Didn't have much to do, so I thought I'd hang out here in the wilderness for a while.* But it's best not to mess around with superficial answers to questions that have been uttered by God himself, questions that invite us into deeper levels of self-awareness. It's best to let the truth pour out—desperation, desire, whatever has driven us to the wilderness and keeps us waiting so far outside our comfort zone.

It is best to just come clean as Elijah does. In a rush of self-disclo-
sure he responds, "I have been very zealous for the LORD, the God of
hosts; for the Israelites have forsaken your covenant, thrown down
your altars, and killed your prophets with the sword. I alone am left,
and they are seeking my life, to take it away."

There it is—the good, the bad, and the ugly. The good Elijah could
see and name in God's presence was that he had been zealous for the
Lord. He *had been* an open and unblocked conduit for the power of
God to come coursing into physical reality in the presence of many
who needed to see it. The bad news was the Israelites had forsaken
God and killed some of his prophets, a frightening admission for
someone whose vocation it was to keep people on track through the
prophetic word. The ugliness Elijah needed to claim as his own was
that he had lost his perspective, he was disillusioned and his faith was
at an all-time low. Rather than remembering the victories he had experienced, all he could remember were the losses. And even though
he was not the only faithful prophet left in Israel, this was how he felt:
"I alone am left, and they are seeking my life to take it away."

This willingness to see ourselves as we are and to name it in God's
presence is at the very heart of the spiritual journey. But it takes time,
time to feel safe enough with ourselves and with God to risk exposing
the tender, unfinished places of the soul. We are so accustomed to being shamed or condemned in the unfinished parts of ourselves that
it is hard to believe there is a place where all of who we are—the
good, the bad and the ugly—will be handled with love and gentle-
ness. Solitude is just such a place, but it takes time to learn to trust it.

This is part of what the waiting is about. It is about becoming safe
enough with God that we are no longer defending ourselves or hiding
ourselves in his presence. It is about waiting for the ego to finally give

up trying to control everything and make it look presentable. It is about accepting the emptiness that comes when we let go of our attempts at image management because we are finally ready to deal in truth, at least to the extent that we are able to bear it. All of this just takes time.

It took me a long time (I won't tell you how long!) to become safe enough with myself and with God to allow the good, the bad and the ugly to come pouring out. But eventually the outer chaos settled down, and I could finally hear God's question as it was addressed to me: *What are you doing here, Ruth?*

I was finally ready to risk an honest answer:

I have been very zealous for the Lord. I've been investing my life in others. I've defended the faith. I've taken risks. I've been very busy loving and serving and leading others, but the truth is, I am empty. Even though I've been really busy with stuff that looks really important, when I am alone with myself I am lonely and sad. To be completely honest, I am angry. I am angry about some of what I have seen and experienced among your people, angry that the Christian life has come up so empty. It scares me to be this angry and this sad. I thought the spiritual life would be something more than this, but now I'm not sure any of it makes much of a difference. It feels like I am the only one.

These are hard admissions; they are the kind that expose us for who we are.

One would think God might try to engage us in conversation at this point or chide us or do something to fix us. One would think he might try to talk us out of what we are experiencing or give an inspiring speech intended to pull us out of the funk we are in. But he

doesn't; at least that's not what he does with Elijah. Rather, he in-
structs Elijah to take his whole self—the good, the bad and the
ugly—and go out and stand on the mountain and wait for the presence of the Lord to pass by.

There seems to be some connection between the willingness to enter into this kind of self-knowledge and true encounter with the
transforming presence of God. But first we must pass through a sea-
son of chaos that can be frightening in its intensity. As Elijah waits
with his whole self open to God, there is a great wind, so strong it
splits mountains and breaks rocks in pieces before the Lord, but the
Lord is not in the wind; and after the wind an earthquake, but the
Lord is not in the earthquake; and after the earthquake a fire, but the
Lord is not in the fire.

I believe there was a literal wind, a literal earthquake, a literal fire.
But I also believe that this elemental chaos is a metaphor for the inner
chaos that surges within when we stay in the presence of the Unchanging Real long enough for pretense and performance and *every
other thing that has bolstered our sense of self* to fall away. When we have
been stripped of external distraction, we face the fact that the deepest
level of chaos is inside us, at our very core. In this place we are buf-
feted by all manner of questions and emotions. False patterns of
thinking and being and doing that have lurked unnoticed under the
surface busyness of our lives are all of sudden *on the surface,* wreaking
havoc on the structures and foundations on which we have built our
identity. Things that seemed sturdy and utterly solid—our sense of
who God is and where he can be found, our sense of ourselves and
how we identify ourselves in this world, our sense of how much we
can control outcomes in our own life and in the lives of others—now
swirl around us in broken pieces, propelled by forces that are clearly
more powerful than we are.

*Am I really worth anything if I'm not out there constantly proving my-
self? Who am I when I am not busy doing things that tell the world who I
am? Why is it so hard to stop the frantic pace of my life even when I know
it's hurting me and those I love? What do I do with this pain and sadness?
What is true and real in my relationship with God and what is merely il-
lusion—things I would like to believe are true but really aren't? Is God really enough to satisfy the loneliness, the emptiness, the longing of my soul?*

These are the questions that have rocked my world in solitude. They
have called into question much of what I was doing. I began to see that
my motives for much of my activity were not as pure and altruistic and
"spiritual" as I had wanted to believe. When these questions came for
the first time, I had to face the fact that much of my hard work and service up to that point had been driven by an effort to please others and
prove my worth to them—particularly those in positions of authority.
Over time I became aware that even though I had a sincere desire to
serve God, there was also a compulsive need to prove myself that re-
sulted in drivenness and constant overcommitment.

It was confusing and frightening to see this and to name it in God's
presence. Even more devastating was the realization that these patterns of relying on performance to prove my worth were so deeply
rooted that I had no idea how to change them. Once I started to see
these patterns for what they were, I wasn't even sure how to function!

Your questions and points of awareness may be different than
mine, but the experience of the chaos they create is the same. All I
can say about this part of the journey is that it is a good thing we took
the time to rest early on. It takes every bit of strength we have gained
in that resting to stand firm in the midst of the storm that is created
by these first glimpses of ourselves as we really are. Perhaps we
glimpse an ego-driven self that is bent on control and image management. Perhaps we see an empty self that is hungry to fill itself with

the approval of others. Perhaps we glimpse the broken self desperately seeking to preserve its identity as one who has it all together. Or maybe we see a wounded self that has spent untold energy seeking healing where healing cannot be found.

I remember a time when my journey into solitude and silence took me to a place of seeing my wounded self more clearly. I was in the process of writing a book on relationships between women and men in the Christian community. At one point I had completed five chapters and decided to take a day in solitude and silence for the sole purpose of reading those chapters to see how I felt about them.

I began the day at 9:00 in the morning, and after an initial period of silence and prayer in which I invited God to show me what I needed to see, I read all five chapters straight through. And guess what? *I hated them!* Taken all together, the tone of the book was angry and strident, relying primarily on preaching and argumentation to get my point across. I noticed that even though the book was meant to appeal to both men and women, it was clearly weighted toward the experiences and perspectives of women without fair representation of the experiences and concerns of men. Furthermore, it seemed like a regurgitation of other people's research and writing rather than offering any fresh insight. With a sinking heart I realized that, as far as I could see, there was nothing that made it worth publishing.

At that point the book served as a mirror reflecting my lack of healing in a very important area. As I looked into that mirror, I saw that my unresolved hurt and anger had seeped into the book. I saw myself as the argumentative and hard-edged person I was, trying to prove myself once again. I saw a person who still hadn't learned how to love—particularly, in this case, my brothers in Christ. I saw someone who was self-absorbed rather than someone who had listened deeply to the stories and experiences of others. This was a devastating awareness. To make matters worse, I was already under contract and had a firm deadline and publication date. To shift the tone and content of the book to something that would be more helpful seemed like a mammoth job. It would require a level of transformation in me that I wasn't sure how to accomplish.

For the better part of that day, all I could do was sit with the truth that this look in the mirror had revealed. I felt as if the book project and I myself had spun out of control, and I had no idea what to do. I simply sat still in the middle of the chaos created by this self-knowledge.

The lunch hour came and went, and I still felt paralyzed by what I now knew. But as I rested through the early afternoon, I began to experience stillness, a sense of trust that I would not be forever lost in the confusion but that I was passing through a difficult place that would somehow be deeply good in the end. Beyond my understanding, I became aware of God with me, as steady and as loving in his intent as he always had been. I even began to have these fraction-of-a-second glimpses of some kind of freedom and healing on the other side of this disturbing morass if I would just stick with it.

And then, somewhere along the way that afternoon, God began to impress upon me the importance of suspending my writing for a time. I sensed him guiding me to take a couple of months to just listen to the men in my life without agenda, without trying to convince them of anything, without concern that they understand me, but rather seeking to understand them. God's instruction was clear. "You have not listened to the men in your life," I could hear him say. "You have been so intent on getting them to listen to you that you have not listened to their stories, their experiences, their concerns. How could this book possibly reflect a male perspective when you have never stopped the flow of your own thoughts long enough to listen? Now is the time for you to take time to listen and trust me with the outcome."

So that's what I did. I stopped writing and set up a series of interviews with male friends, relatives and coworkers to just listen to their stories, concerns, fears and issues. And thus began a several-month process of entering more deeply into friendship and conversation with men that had a profound and life-transforming effect on me. These conversations softened me, challenged me and invited me into the risks of loving rather than relying so heavily on intellectual skill and cognitive debate.

Then, from a softer and more loving place, I wrote a sixth chapter, included it with the other five and sent them all off to the publisher. A few weeks later my editor called and said, "I didn't much like the first five chapters, but I really liked the sixth one." She did not know everything that had transpired to cause that kind of change, but I did. And thus began the arduous but deeply fulfilling task of reworking the first half of the book and writing the second half of the book in the spirit of learning and change that self-knowledge in God's presence had brought forth.

When we find ourselves in the rugged terrain of deeper self-knowledge, we may feel very alone, we may feel ashamed, we may feel as if we are the only ones who have ever had to experience such a soul-shaking experience. For some of us—especially those of us who have been Christians for a long time—the view of the self that we gain in solitude is shocking. We thought we were better off than that! We thought we had come farther. By now we have a lot riding on our ability to keep these false expressions of ourselves under cover. What's more, we're not sure there is any other self than the self we have constructed in reaction to the wounds and pains of our life. We have identified with this adapted self for so long and so relied on its energy to propel us forward that we don't know who we will be if this self dies. It is the only self we have ever known. Suddenly it is a very precarious cliff we are standing on, this place where God has instructed us to stand and wait.

It is comforting—and absolutely essential—to know that this is a very predictable place on the spiritual journey. In classic Christian tradition it is known as the process of illumination (waking up to what reality actually is) and purgation (being stripped of that within us that is false). If we are unaware of this stage, we might fear that we are somehow falling off the spiritual path rather than trusting it as one of the most important passages of the journey.

The purgative passage is characterized by a fierce stripping away, a dying to the only self we have ever known. Intellectual categories, relational and behavioral patterns, even theological beliefs and spiritual practices that have served us in the past begin to crack and crumble. There is a profound sense of vulnerability and disorientation. We feel like a mess—completely out of control.

This is the place that Isaiah came to when he saw the glory of the Lord and his immediate and gut-wrenching response was, "Woe is me! I am lost, for I am a man of unclean lips, and I live among a people of unclean lips" (Is 6:5). It is the place where David vomits up his anger and hatred in prayer to God (Ps 139) and invites God to search him and show him a truer way. It is the process that began for Saul when we was blinded by the light of God's presence on the Damascus Road and sat in darkness for three days until the "scales fell from his eyes, and his sight was restored" (Acts 9:18). During those three days, he saw himself for who he was and responded deeply to the invitations of God in his life. He was changed forever.

But the seeing was not a one-time event for Saul/Paul, and it is not a one-time event for us either. Further along his spiritual journey, with great vulnerability, Paul shares the pain and feeling of impotence he experiences as he sees the old self fighting and struggling once again with the truer "inmost self" that wants so desperately to respond to life in the Spirit. It is a painful seeing and a place where only the grace of God can accomplish what is needed (see Rom 7).

At first we try to grasp at any handhold that might keep us from falling into the abyss of our nothingness. We hold on to whatever we can for as long as we can, but eventually we must let go. This feels like too much, given the amount of letting go that we have already done. After all, we have already let go of our dependence on noise and words and activity and people. We have let go of our strong identification with the outer trappings of roles and responsibilities to define ourselves. We have experienced the inner void and peered into its blackness. But now there is one more invitation: to let go of the very last handhold—the handhold of the self we have created in response to the wounds of our life in an imperfect world—and free-fall into what seems like the utter silence of the void.

> The process of being conformed to the image of Christ takes place primarily at the point of our unlikeness to Christ's image. God is present to us in the most destructive aspects of our cultural captivity. God is involved with us in the most imprisoning bondage of our brokenness. God meets us in those places of our lives that are most alienated from God.
>
> ROBERT MULHOLLAND, *INVITATION TO A JOURNEY*

It feels like the bravest thing we have ever done—bungee jumping for the soul, if you will. We are truly out of control, far beyond the known, the safe, the familiar. Beyond the personal pampering many in our culture have come to identify as solitude, we begin to understand that, as Henry Nouwen says,

> solitude is not a private therapeutic place. Rather it is the place of conversion, the place where the old self dies and the new self is born. . . . In solitude I get rid of my scaffolding: no friends to talk with, no telephone calls to make, no meetings to attend, no music to entertain, no books to distract, just me—naked, vulnerable, weak, sinful, deprived, broken—nothing. It is this nothingness that I have to face in my solitude, a nothingness so dreadful that everything in me wants to run to my friends, my work, my distractions so that I can forget my nothingness and make myself believe that I am worth something. . . .
>
> I try to run from the dark abyss of my nothingness and restore my false self in all its vainglory. The task is to persevere in my solitude, to stay in my cell until all my seductive visitors get tired of pounding on my door and leave me alone. . . .
>
> The struggle is real because the danger is real. It is the danger of living the whole of our life as one long defense against the reality of our condition.

Self-knowledge does not always have to be this earth-shattering; sometimes it is a much simpler awareness. For instance, one woman shared that as she entered into solitude and silence one morning, she heard God say to her, "Sometimes you're not very nice to people." This revelation was stunning in its clarity, simplicity and accuracy. It offered her guidance for knowing exactly what needed attention in her life. The point is that on any given day, God might visit us with something as simple as this insight or something more far-reaching, and there is a sting or perhaps a deeper sorrow.

But this seeing, as painful as it is, is really a gift from God. It ushers us in to the godly grief that leads to repentance and eventually our salvation (2 Cor 7:10). It is a sign that God is illuminating our darkness so that we can live in the light of his love and freedom. It is best not to resist God's illuminating work—even though resistance is our most natural response—but to give in to the process, trusting that there is a truer self waiting to be recognized and breathed into life by the Spirit of God.

But this waiting is not to be confused with passivity. Waiting on God in the silent places of the soul is an active waiting that contains a seed of expectancy and hope. We wait with the kind of anticipation a night watchman feels as he waits for the morning sun to signal the end of his watch. No matter how many hours of darkness he has to wait through, the watchman knows from experience that morning will come. He is alert to the dangers of the night while every fiber of his being leans toward that coming. His eyes have become practiced at recognizing the first ray of sunlight on the horizon (see Ps 130:5-6).

This is how we wait for God—with longing, with expectancy, with alert awareness, our whole self straining to catch the earliest possible glimpse of this God who comes. In so doing, we open ourselves to the possibility of being met by God in the silence that follows the storm.

> The LORD was not in the wind . . . the LORD was not in the earthquake . . . the LORD was not in the fire; and after the fire a sound of sheer silence.

Practice

As you enter into silence today, take several deep breaths as a way of settling into these moments and becoming aware of God's presence with you—closer to you than your breath.

When you feel ready, hear God ask you the question he asked

Elijah. *What are you doing here, _____?* Sit quietly with the question, allowing it to penetrate all the way to the core of your being.

Allow your response to this question to emerge from your heart without trying to edit it. You may want to write your response in your journal, you may want to respond with spoken words, or you may need to just experience the emotion that comes. The point is to communicate with God as honestly as you can about what is drawing you deeper and deeper into solitude right now. It may be serious and weighty, but it doesn't have to be. Most recently when God asked me this question in solitude, it did not stir up the chaos I described earlier. This time my honest answer was:

> I am here because I have been very zealous for the Lord, for what appears to be his purposes. Today there is no sadness, no discouragement, not even the familiar loneliness. There is this sense that everything is as it should be, but sometimes my zealousness gets the better of me and I push for what is not quite ready to come. I feel a familiar frenetic quality to my activity that indicates I am not as grounded as I would like to be. I am here because I need to find the ground of my being again.

For right now, let it be enough to say what is true about you and then just wait in God's presence.

10

Pure Presence

> Solitude eventually offers a quiet gift of grace, a gift that
> comes whenever we are able to face ourselves honestly: the
> gift of acceptance, of compassion, for who we are as we are.
> As we allow ourselves to be known in solitude, we discover
> that we are known by love. Beyond the pain of self-discovery
> there is a love that does not condemn us but calls us to itself.
> This love receives us as we are.
>
> PARKER PALMER

To stay on the journey into solitude and silence now is to stay with the experience of seeing ourselves as we are in God's presence, as challenging as it is. In solitude we stop defending against the reality of our condition, we give up our attempts to control the outcomes of our journey because we can finally see it is quite beyond our ability to control. We let go of our attachment to the pieces of ourselves that we have allowed to define us. We endure the storm created by the old self as it frantically tries to maintain control.

During this part of the journey we may also experience grief as we begin to see all the ways we cut ourselves off from the love that our heart longs for. We may become aware that the pain we have experienced is not merely the result of evil "out there" but also a result of patterns of sin and brokenness that have hardened in and around our own heart.

While these patterns may have developed in reaction to very real traumas and enigmas, they do not serve the journey that God is inviting us to now. We need to take responsibility for having allowed these patterns to shape our lives and responses to others, so that we can choose a different way within the intimacy and safety of our love relationship with God.

Accompanying this self-awareness is a desperate desire for healing and communion that is painful in its intensity. To truly see, with the eyes of the soul, our need for transformation at the very core of our being elicits a longing that is beyond words. This part of the spiritual process is so demanding that we may be sorely tempted to turn back. The problem with this possibility is that there is no place to go back to once we have seen ourselves for who we are, enslaved to patterns of relating and being and doing that are ultimately antithetical to the life we are seeking. Where do we go once we realize that we have been living in bondage and we have glimpsed the way of freedom? The only real option is to face it bravely, knowing that truth-seeing will ultimately lead us into freedom. This is all we can do. It does no good to try and fix what we see. It is useless to make excuses for what we see. It is cowardly to blame others for what we see. And denying what we see just puts us right back in the mess. The only thing we can do is to keep our whole selves turned toward God even as we endure the grief and unsettledness that the seeing brings.

But if we are faithful to the seeing, to the grief, to the letting go . . . if to the best of our ability we cease striving, stop kicking and fighting . . . if we release our grasping and clinging . . .

All of a sudden it becomes very quiet.

At first the quiet may feel like just another place of emptiness. We may even feel a sense of dread or fear that we are going to be judged or punished for parts of ourselves we have now brought into the light of day.

But if we stay in this moment, eventually—like Elijah—we begin to notice that this silence is qualitatively different from the emptiness we experienced before. The silence that comes after the chaos is pregnant with the presence of God.

Like Elijah, we may be surprised that at a point of painful self-awareness God does not chide us or scold us or give us a motivational speech inspiring us to pull ourselves together and get back at it. No, in Elijah's willingness to be there as he was—open and raw and receptive—and in our willingness as well, God grants a most powerful experience of his loving presence.

This silence is unlike all other silences, for it is full of a Presence that makes itself known as a subtle stirring in the soul, a gentle blowing, a quiet whisper. For some there may even be a physical sensation, a vibration, a vision or a voice.

At first we may not know what it is. We may not trust that God has come *to us* in a way that we can finally experience in the very cells of our being. Perhaps we have assumed that such experiences of the Presence of God are reserved for others who are more spiritual than we think of ourselves as being. *It's probably nothing,* we say to ourselves. *Perhaps it is a figment of my imagination. Or perhaps this is something I should be afraid of.*

It takes time and experience to recognize this God who reaches out and seeks to communicate and commune with us. Who knows what it was that caused Elijah to recognize God's presence in the sound of sheer silence? But the fruit of Elijah's willingness to remain open to God in the midst of inner chaos created by self-knowledge was that he came to understand *through experience* that he was loved and valued just as much when he was alone, exhausted and not performing very well as he was when he was standing on a mountain top calling down the fire of God in front of heathen prophets and fickle followers.

When Elijah experienced "the sound of sheer silence" that was full of the Presence of God, there was no need for words or any kind of cognitive response. He wrapped his face in his mantle—a sign of absolute reverence—and he went out and just stood in that Presence. He let the Presence wash over him.

I know of no better response.

The fruit of our waiting and willingness in that silence, ironically, becomes one of the fullest experiences of the spiritual life. Finally I am knowing in the depth of my experience that God is God *for me* and *with me* and *in me*. In the original languages of the Bible there are much better and more nuanced words for describing the kind of knowing that is so far beyond our cognitive, informational knowing. The Old and New Testament writers describe a kind of knowledge "that unites the subject with object." It is a full participation in the truth or the reality being explored. It is the difference between hearing or reading about a person and actually becoming an intimate friend, between saying "I love you" to a spouse and actually making love. It is the difference between saying you believe someone or

> *The deepest level of communication is not communication but communion. It is wordless. It is beyond words, and beyond speech, and it is beyond concept.*
>
> THOMAS MERTON

something is trustworthy and actually trusting them with something that is important to you. It is full participation in the reality of God and giving ourselves over to that reality.

This is the most important kind of knowing in the human experience, and it comes only as we are quiet enough to let the faithful presence of God hold us in our brokenness until our brokenness is healed by love. All other kinds of knowing merely set the stage for this. As painful as it is, the process of seeing ourselves as we are and allowing God to do his work in the place that needs it most is full of grace. It offers the opportunity to break out of patterns of thinking and believing which distort our reality, condition our responses to others and prevent us from living as a free self in God. It offers us the opportunity to give ourselves over to the One who loves us as we are and yet loves us too much to let us stay as we are.

But what is left after we have been stripped of the false self, when the tear has gone so deep that we fear that our very essence has been ripped away? Well, this is the part that some of us find hard to believe. We have identified for so long with the illusions of the sinful, wounded self that we can't imagine there is anything truer about

Transformation is the process of God's recreating our very selves. In the last phase [radical transformation] we are completely out of control, we are no longer in charge. God has taken over and is working on levels of our being we cannot get to.

The Divine Physician is performing deep spiritual surgery on us. The surgery is getting to the root of the "stuff" inside us that prevents us from seeing and hearing the gospel. All the phases of transformation are not done through our strategies. They are done to us because

we are open to remaining in the presence of God.

CARL ARICO, *A TASTE OF SILENCE*

us than that. We have not yet glimpsed the essential self that is a created good brought into being by God himself, known by God long before we were brought into physical form. It is a self that is fearfully and wonderfully made with a purpose uniquely suited to the way it was formed (Ps 139).

This self is smaller, in one sense, than the ego identity, because it does not need to be big in order to prove itself to the world. This self is truer, because it does not rely on image management to find acceptance in the world. This self is softer, because it does not rely on hardened defense structures to keep itself safe in the world. This self is freer, because it knows itself to be finally and ultimately held safely in a Love that is unchangeable and real.

This Love does not lose track of us no matter what dark places we must walk into. It is a Love deeper than any abyss that we might fall into. It is a Love with the power to heal any brokenness we might encounter.

This Love eventually becomes a bedrock of settledness at the core of our being. It is worth any price we have to pay to find it.

Practice

As you enter the silence today, take several deep breaths as a way of settling into the quiet intimacy that you and God have been learning to share. Allow yourself to feel the safety of this time, this place, this Presence. Take a few moments to just enjoy it.

As you are quiet in God's presence, reflect on your response to God's question at the end of chapter nine: *What are you doing here,*

_____? Is there any self-awareness that has come to you in answering this question? Is there any area of your life where God is illuminating your need to be transformed?

As you reflect on the reading today, notice the place(s) where you found yourself saying, "That's exactly where I am!" Perhaps you are in a preawareness stage: you know something is not quite right, but you're not sure what it is. Perhaps you are in the midst of seeing yourself as you've never seen yourself before. Maybe you at are at the point of desperation, finally willing to lie back and let God do the work of stripping away the knottiest layers of the false self. You may even be experiencing the silence that is full of the Presence of God, and you're not quite sure if you can trust it.

Whatever is happening in the silence today, just stay in it without trying to run from it. Tell God what you are experiencing, and ask him if there is anything he wants you to do in response. Invite him to take initiative with you in regard to whatever you are seeing, and follow any promptings that come. God has an uncanny ability to bring exactly what it is we need, right when we are ready to receive it.

Close your time in prayer today by reciting the Lord's Prayer out loud if possible. Particularly if you are needing to let go of one of the handholds of your false self, envision yourself joining with Christ as he prays this prayer with his disciples. Allow the praying of this prayer to anchor you in the Unchanging Reality of God's kingdom, even though it feels as if everything around you is shifting and falling away.

11

Receiving Guidance

Under the silent, watchful eye of the Holy One we are all
standing, whether we know it or not. And in that Center, in
that holy Abyss where the eternal dwells at the base of our
being, our programs, our gifts to God, our offerings of duties
performed again and again are revised in their values. . . .
If we center down and live in that Holy Silence which is dearer
than life, and take our life program into the silent places of
the heart with complete openness, ready to renounce
according to God's leading, then many of the things we are
doing will lose their vitality for us.

THOMAS KELLY

Many of us enter into prayer and quiet because we are desperate
for guidance in some area of our life. Like Elijah, we may even have
reached a place of impasse: some aspect of our life clearly isn't working, but we have no idea what to do differently. Because we are Christian people, we really do want to figure out the will of God so we can
do it. We want to get it right!

How surprising it is to find that our deepest need is to know we can never fall out of that unconditional love within which we live and move and have our being. Beyond formulaic approaches designed to harness God for our purposes, we learn to relinquish control and simply be present to the One whose presence is the bedrock of our being. Given time, we experience that loving Presence as our ultimate reality. We learn in the very cells of our being that this Reality never changes; it is only that our awareness of it is sometimes dulled by the noise and clutter of life.

This reorientation to the ultimate reality of God's love and goodness is an important first step to receiving guidance. For only when we know the love of God in a deep, experiential way can we be truly open and receptive to his will. Without this knowing it is hard to listen openly for the still, small voice of God, because we are afraid of what we may hear. We're afraid we may hear the voice of a killjoy God who is just looking for a chance to force us into doing what we most dread. When it comes right down to it, many of us do not believe that God's intentions toward us are deeply good; instead we live in fear that that if we really trusted him, he might withhold something good from us.

No wonder that Dallas Willard says,

> The first objective [in the discipleship process] is to bring apprentices to the point where they dearly love and constantly delight in that "heavenly Father" made real to earth in Jesus and are quite certain that there is no "catch," no limit, to the goodness of his intentions or his power to carry them out.

When we are settled in God's love at the core of our being, the waters of the soul become much clearer. We glimpse a more authentic self with truer and more essential gifts to bring to the world than those wrestled out of the unconscious striving of the false self. These gifts come from our created essence, the self that God knew and saw and formed for a purpose that existed before the foundations of the earth (Ps 139). We learn to recognize the gifts and dynamics of the authentic self because they are *qualitatively* different from those that come primarily from human striving; they come forth in peace and humility and strength to meet the deep needs of our world. When we grow quiet enough to notice the difference between these two aspects of ourselves, true spiritual guidance can begin to unfold in our life.

It is interesting that Elijah never asked for guidance; guidance simply came in the context of his willingness to be with God in utter openness and vulnerability. Something in the willingness to stop the flow of his own words and listen in silence opened up space for the One who longs to speak and offer guidance for our next steps and knottiest questions. Like a wise and loving parent who waits for a self-sufficient or willful teenager to come to the end of her own wisdom and express openness to being guided, God loves us enough to wait for the teachable moment.

After Elijah endured the ferocity of his own inner chaos and stood still long enough so the presence of God became palpable, the question came again. "What are you doing here, Elijah?" Or, "How are you doing now, Elijah?"

Surprisingly enough, Elijah's answer was still the same. "I have been very zealous for the LORD, the God of hosts; for the Israelites have forsaken your covenant, thrown down your altars, and killed your prophets with the sword. I alone am left, and they are seeking my life, to take it away."

God then gave Elijah very practical instructions about appointing new kings and also choosing a prophet to eventually replace him. Implicit in this interchange was a gracious and realistic acknowledgment that Elijah was deeply worn out and needed to do life a bit differently. God's intention was not for Elijah to stay in solitude forever; it was that he return to his prophetic ministry rested and recalibrated through the wisdom he had received. Now Elijah had guidance for how to go back more wisely with consideration for his true limitations. He was able to reenter life in the company of others with staying power that sustained him until the end of his life on earth.

But what about us normal folks who don't typically carry on audible conversations with God while standing on the side of a mountain? The fact that we can't see God makes it easy to slip into a pattern of doing all the talking ourselves. Is it too much to expect that God might speak back to us, not only with expressions of love but with guidance that is trustworthy and wise? Is it grandiose to believe God might actually interact with me in such a personal and timely way? And if I do hear something, how do I know it is God's voice and not just my own thoughts masquerading as something more spiritual? How do I know it is not a figment of my imagination, a manifestation of my wishful thinking?

One of the basic assumptions of the Christian life is that God does communicate with us through the Holy Spirit. The rhythm of speaking and listening we call communication is at the heart of any real relationship—including our relationship with God. Late in his life on earth, Jesus told his disciples that it was to our advantage that he go away, for then the Holy Spirit could come and be present with us as a counselor and adviser, One who could guide us into truth right here, right now, as we need it.

The capacity to recognize the voice of God through the ministry of the Holy Spirit arises out of friendship with God that is sustained through prayer, silent listening and attentiveness to all that is going on outside us, inside us, and between us and God. Through practice and experience we become familiar with the tone of God's voice, the content of his communications with us and his unique way of addressing us. We learn to recognize God's voice just as we recognize the voice of a loved one on the other end of the phone. There is a place deep inside each of us where God's Spirit witnesses with our spirit about things that are true (Rom 8:16). It takes experience and practice to learn to recognize the communication that goes on in that place.

I remember one of the first times I began to recognize God's voice offering guidance in times of solitude and silence, particularly through the ability to distinguish between the true and the false self. I was in seminary preparing to enter into ordained ministry, a dearly held dream. Because I was a mother with three young children, I was taking one class at a time, and at the end of five years I was about halfway through.

Although I still often struggled through the actual moments of silence, I could tell I was starting to calm down. Instead of the chaos that had been the primary characteristic of my inner life, there was a quiet center forming in me, a place of stillness from which I could perceive things more clearly and respond with what was truly called for in the moment.

It was into this place of stillness that I took a serious question. I had begun to sense God's calling into the ministry of spiritual direction, and I was also considering a staff position in the area of spiritual formation at a church that I loved. These were very exciting possibilities.

The problem was that my seminary coursework offered little in the areas in which I needed training. I had already taken the only course in spiritual formation the seminary offered, and I knew I needed more. I felt caught between my clear need for the master of divinity degree—the degree generally expected of those entering into pastoral ministry—and my awareness that this degree did not provide the coursework needed for the ministry to which I was being called.

As I took my quandary into the stillness, I noticed that I was processing this decision with new freedom. First of all, although I was aware of potential losses and gains inherent in the decision I was facing, I did not feel inordinately threatened by the possibility that I might not finish my degree. In earlier times I could easily have panicked at the idea of letting go of a plan I had made and would have clung to the importance of gaining credibility through a traditional credential. But through the practices of solitude and silence, the compulsions of the false self, while still present, had settled down considerably. I could more easily consider relinquishing my need to prove something to others through a particular degree. Instead of working hard to figure things out on a cognitive level and forcing a solution that made sense from a human point of view, I began to sense what God was calling forth in my life so I could simply join him in it.

In this case, clear circumstances, desires and affirmations from others indicated that something different was emerging in my life from what I had planned. Rather than defending against hearing God's voice because I was afraid of what he might say, I was certain of God's love and good intentions toward me. This helped me to trust him in the moment and listen and wait for clear direction.

It was especially helpful to notice subtle differences between the motivations of the false self and God's invitations to the true self. Because I had been growing increasingly safe in God's presence, I could handle God raising this very tough question: "Are you enamored with having the letters M.Div. after your name as a way of proving yourself, or are you willing to choose the truer desire to be shaped for what's at the core of who you are—even if your qualifications will not be immediately recognizable to the world?"

This question helped me distinguish between the dynamics of the false self and those of the true self. Being aware of the differences helped me observe that finishing seminary had lost some of its attraction because there was a truer path to be followed. Rather than being overly concerned about how all the pieces of my life would fit together and whether I'd be respected as a woman in ministry without the M.Div., I was satisfied with recognizing the next step that was clear and trusting it.

It has been five years since I made the decision to choose a different path of study and experiential learning, and it stands as one of the best vocational decisions I have ever made, even though it didn't make a lot of sense at the time. The years of training I have received in one-to-one spiritual direction, group spiritual direction and retreat leadership have been exactly what I have needed to carry out the ministry to which I have been called.

As I followed this step and many others after it, I have found that the path God is leading me on—spiritually, relationally, vocationally—is somehow truer and more deeply satisfying than any other way of choosing and making decisions I have experienced. Contained within each faithful response to God's guidance is the seed of the next possibility.

I have also discovered that there is a place in any true discernment process where some aspect of the path laid out for us defies human wisdom. God's wisdom is so far beyond us that it feels like foolishness (1 Cor 1:18—2:16). Sometimes great faith is required to follow God's wisdom. Once again we are faced with the limitations of the human mind and our need to trust, yet again, that which is beyond ourselves.

The unfolding of discernment in our lives is never over. Recently I have again become aware of a familiar stirring: the desire to serve a little church as an ordained minister. Sometimes I feel a longing to administer the sacraments out of the reverence and understanding that has grown within me over the last few years, or I notice a desire to speak pastorally into the ongoing life of a community, or I feel passion to bring gifts of listening and discernment to the leadership of a local gathering of believers.

It is a very quiet and simple desire, but it is still there. It is a sweet desire that resides in a very authentic place in me. I do not know what will come of that desire and whether it will involve finishing what I started all those years ago. I do know there is a wonderful freedom that comes from paying attention to those desires without needing to figure everything out, but rather being willing to simply watch for the work of God.

Receiving guidance involves trusting that there are some desires that are very true because they issue from the essence of our created self, the unformed substance God knew before the foundations of the earth and called into being in his time. These desires are the ones God promises to meet if we follow every next step that's clear without being overly concerned about how he will bring it all together (Ps 37:4-5; Is 43:1). What is most important is our moment-by-moment response to the promptings of the Spirit as we become more practiced at recognizing them.

At the very heart of the discernment process is an ability to pay at-

tention not only to the obvious—circumstances, the clear meaning of
pertinent Scriptures, the advice of friends who are wise in the Lord,
the wisdom contained in our faith tradition—but also to the inner
dynamics that give us clues as to whether the step we are considering
will nurture life in us: the life of Christ lived in and through our most
authentic self. Ignatius, the great
saint best known for articulating
this aspect of the discernment
process, identifies these clues as
experiences of *consolation* and *des-
olation*. Consolation is the interior
movement of the heart that gives
us a deep sense of life-giving connection with God, others and our
authentic self in God. It is the
sense that all is right with the
world, that I am free to be given
over to God and to love even in
moments of pain and crisis. Deso-
lation is the loss of a sense of God's
presence. We feel out of touch with God, with others and with our
most authentic self. It is the experience of being off-center, full of tur-
moil, confusion and maybe even rebellion.

> *Obedience is indispensable. Not to a static code, however helpful it may be at times. But obedience to God, who is present with us in every situation and is speaking to us all the time. Every obedience, however small (if any obedience is ever small), quickens our sensitivity to him and our capacity to understand him and so makes more real our sense of his presence.*
>
> ALBERT EDWARD DAY, *THE CAPTIVATING PRESENCE*

God's will for us is generally for us to do more of that which gives
us life (Jn 10:10) and to turn away from activities that drain life from
us and debilitate us. Most significant decisions—even those that require us to choose between two ostensibly good options like the
M.Div. and training in spiritual direction—involve the ability to notice what brings a sense of life and freedom to the true self as we experience ourselves in God. In Deuteronomy God addresses the whole

company of Israel and says, "See, I have set before you life and pros-
perity, death and adversity. . . . Choose life so that you and your de-
scendants may live" (Deut 30:15, 19). The wisdom that enables us to
choose life is not something we will find somewhere far away in
heaven or across the ocean; God says this knowing is very near to
us—in our mouths and in our hearts for us to notice and observe
(Deut 30:11-14).

As we make it our habit to notice and move toward that which
gives us life, receiving guidance becomes routine in day-to-day life as
well as in the larger questions. The habit of discernment keeps us in
touch with the movement of God's Spirit within ourselves and in the
lives of others, so that we can make choices congruent with the life
the Spirit is bringing forth. Then we can draw upon understanding
and awareness gained through the habit of discernment to inform
our larger life decisions.

The practices of solitude and silence give us a place for paying attention to our inner dynamics, to our circumstances and relationships, and to the dynamics of our relationship with God so that
guidance can come as needed. Elijah was wise not to grab for guidance but to simply be open to it.

One of the most reassuring aspects of the Holy Spirit's ministry is
that the Holy Spirit guides us into truth *as we are able to bear it* (Jn
16:12-13). While certain decisions may feel urgent and we earnestly
seek God's guidance for them, it is good to trust God's timing, for he
knows what we can handle.

The aim of our search for guidance is not merely to improve our
own life; it is to enhance our participation in God's work in ways that
are congruent with our truest self in God. Over time, the reorientation of our mind and our heart and our will to the unchanging reality
of God brings about a transformation that enables us to prove with

our whole life that the will of God is good and acceptable and deeply right for us and for our world.

Practice

Take a few moments to allow your body to settle into a comfortable yet alert position. Take several deep breaths as a way of entering into the silence and making yourself present to the One who is always present with you.

One way to discern God's activity and guidance is to pay attention to what gives us a sense of life and what seems to cut us off from a sense of life. As we become more practiced at noticing these dynamics without judging them, we can be more discerning about choosing what is life-giving in ordinary moments and in the larger decisions.

In your time of silent listening today, ask God to bring to your heart a moment in the last couple of days for which you were most grateful. When were you most able to give and receive love? Which moment seemed to have the most life in it for you?

Ask God to bring to your heart a moment in the last couple of days for which you were *least* grateful. When were you least able to give and receive love? Which moment seemed to drain life from you?

What wisdom, insight or further questions seem to arise from your awareness of moments that were life-giving and moments that were draining? Is there any way God may be guiding you to choose more of what gives you life?

12

For the Sake of Others

Let him who cannot be alone beware of community. . . .
Let him who is not in community beware of being alone.

DIETRICH BONHOEFFER

As we begin experiencing God's presence in solitude, we may find our desire for God and the joy of being with him in this way to be a bit overwhelming. After a time it seemed I just couldn't get enough, and I became a little frightened. I wondered if I would ever be able to fully reengage with people again. Or would I always be wishing to go off by myself? Was I becoming a narcissistic navel-gazer? Was I hopelessly selfish, endlessly needy? Would I ever be good for anything practical again?

Once again my performance anxieties stirred as I compared myself to others who were able to turn out more "real work" than I could as I learned to maintain rhythms of solitude and silence. I wondered if I would ever be capable of producing again. I wondered if I would ever even *care* about producing as much as I had cared about it before. I wished I could probe Elijah's experience a bit more to see if he ever had similar concerns, having journeyed so far from prominence and productivity to a place of deep quiet and hiddenness. Did he, too, wonder if and when he would ever go back to life in the company of others?

For a while I tried to keep these fears and questions to myself. In the midst of the high-performance cultures in which I lived and worked and worshiped, it was embarrassing to acknowledge such a voracious desire for silence and solitude. I was afraid people would question my ability to produce along the lines they were measuring. I was afraid of becoming irrelevant in a world that measures relevance by output and being out front.

At the same time, I realized I was like a starving child who is given a bowl of rice or oatmeal, her first real food in long time. The child is so hungry that once she realizes where the food is dispensed, she can't help hanging around that place. Once she receives her first portion, she grabs it and shovels it into her mouth without stopping to be polite, without slowing down enough to get it all in her mouth, without caring that she is slurping and spilling it down the front of her dress. It's not a pretty sight.

The good news is that eventually it does the job. The emptiness gets filled, so that sooner or later the child can look up from the bowl, wipe her mouth and speak to the people around her. Now that she is satiated she can engage with others on the basis of something besides her hunger and her fear that there wouldn't be enough.

I now know I am not the only one who has become so hungry for true "soul food" that I couldn't seem to get enough. As I have guided others in initial experiences with solitude and silence, often they too are ambushed by the intensity and insatiable quality of their desire. Sometimes they return from their first several hours in real silence, and with a bit of embarrassment (and sometimes a tear sliding down the cheek) they whisper, "Can I ask you something?"

"Sure."

"When it was time to come back, I didn't want to come back. I've never experienced God loving me like that before. I didn't want to leave that place where God was so real to me. I don't want to talk and I don't want anyone to talk to me. Is that normal?"

I'm not sure I know what "normal" is in all these matters of the soul, but I do know many of us have no idea how starving we are, and that is one reason the invitation to solitude and silence holds so much ambivalence. Some of us are so far into the later stages of spiritual starvation that we don't know what it is to be full and well. We have been feeding for so long on the emptiness of words and noise and activity that our soul is emaciated, but like an anorexic teen, we are past the point of desiring real food. The soul-nourishing substance of solitude holds no appeal. We look in the mirror and think that the ninety-five-pound bag of bones we see there is attractive. So even when the opportunity for solitude is there we don't choose it.

Others of us are aware of our hunger and have been for so long that when we find ourselves in the presence of real spiritual food we are frantic with fear that we will never get enough after so much emptiness.

Either way, this is pretty scary stuff. All we can do is trust that the process of receiving nourishment will eventually lead us to a place of being able to give out of fullness.

Something about the process of having our emptiness filled in solitude eventually does enable us to engage with those around us on the basis of fullness rather than need. This is another place where we might need help from a good spiritual director, for this process should not be rushed. The timing is different for all of us. However, if we relax and trust God's initiative in the spiritual process, eventually something new begins to shimmer around the edges of our lives and relationships. A different capacity for being present to others in love comes upon us, almost imperceptibly at first. Far beyond the familiar territory of "ought" and "should," we may notice a spontaneous and surprising desire to find a way to bring some of what we are experiencing in God's presence to others. There is no fanfare to herald such profound inner changes, just a willingness to give ourselves to it.

One night I began to see a glimmer of something new and good for others emerging from my experiences in solitude. It was a beautiful summer evening, the windows and doors were all open, and our home and yard were full of the kind of energy that only a group of lively junior high schoolers could bring. No matter that it was getting late, I was trying to meet a writing deadline and tomorrow was a full day of work; on this night our daughter Bethany and about twenty of her closest friends had come together for an evening of spontaneous "hanging out" at our home. Some were in the backyard playing volleyball, others were on the street shooting hoops, another contingency played pool in the basement, and always there was someone traipsing past my office for a drink or a snack.

My initial reaction to this scenario was irritation. Couldn't I just get a break here? Couldn't I get a little peace and quiet so I could get something done? This was not a new feeling for me; it is who I am when left to myself. All too often, I have responded to my life in the company of others with this kind of frustration, bent on getting my own way and shaping my environment to my own wants and needs. In fact, the awareness of my self-centeredness was one of the things that had sent me on the quest for deeper levels of transformation in the first place.

But on this night I found myself finally ready to ask a different kind of question. Rather than asking how I could manipulate my environment to get what I wanted, the question came, *Is there anything from my experiences of fullness in God these days that I can bring to this moment, to these children?* I wasn't asking the question out of the "guilty mom" place. I was asking it because everything in me ached to give some good gift to these teenagers. But how?

I remembered Julian of Norwich's wonderful statement about being present to God when in the company of others: "I look at God, I look at you, and I keep looking at God." Although I had often prayed for others in this way during times of solitude, on that night I decided to try it in the midst of a very ordinary moment of my life as a busy mom in a houseful of kids, facing deadlines and long workdays, a moment that is repeated over and over again these days. I thought, *If my experiences in solitude and silence don't make a difference in this real-life moment, then I'm not sure any of this is worth much.*

So I looked at God. Sitting in front of my computer trying to bang out an article, tired, kids coming and going from every door . . . I turned inward to that place of quiet where I had grown accustomed to meeting God and asked him to give me sacred eyes—set-apart eyes to see and feel and know spiritual reality in this moment.

Then as I turned my eyes to the children, I began to see and feel things that were a bit uncharacteristic for me. Rather than being frustrated by the desire to be alone so I could write, I was filled with gratitude that these young people had chosen to be in a home where parents are present, expending their youthful energy in life-affirming ways. Rather than wishing my home were quiet, I began experiencing the noise and activity as the energy of youthful spirit, and I was drawn to it, filled by it. Rather than experiencing their comings and goings and curious questions as interruptions, I started noticing how beautiful and distinct each one was, and I was enlivened by the privilege of interacting with them.

After looking with sacred eyes at these children, I looked back at God, and I sensed his love for them filling my own heart. A deep, beyond-words kind of prayer welled up, a prayer that somehow they would be blessed by the bits and pieces of our togetherness.

Rather than the tiredness of one more evening of parental responsibility, being present to God in this moment somehow graced my heart with love and renewed energy and wonder. I touched a spiritual dynamic that was beyond my own ability to produce. In the midst of external noise and chaos, I was present to God in the company of others, and I was changed by it.

I had not moved beyond solitude; rather, by God's grace I brought the quietness of my solitude right into the present moment. I was learning, through experience and experimentation, that solitude does not consist only in creating perfect conditions outside myself in a retreat center, a church or a devotional corner; the quietness of solitude and silence was becoming an inner condition within which I was able to recognize and respond to the stirrings, the voice, the very Presence of God himself.

And so the practices of solitude and silence do, in time, bring us full circle—back into life in the human community. Whether we have been away for a half an hour of solitude, had an extended retreat time or have dropped completely out of sight for a while, God, in his time, does eventually bring us back to the life he has given us. Perhaps nothing in our external circumstances has changed, but *we have changed,* and that's what our world needs more than anything.

Without pressing or pushing or trying to do a great altruistic deed, we discover that much that happens in solitude and silence ends up being "for others"—as paradoxical as that may seem. Our speech patterns are refined by the discipline of silence, because growing self-awareness enables us to choose more truly the words we say. Rather than speech that issues from subconscious needs to impress, to put others in their place, to compete, to control and manipulate, to repay hurt with hurt, we now notice our inner dynamics and choose to speak from a different place, a place of love, trust and true wisdom that God is cultivating within us. Over time we become safer for other seeking souls, because we are able to be with them and the issues they are dealing with without being hooked by our own anxieties and fears. We are comfortable with our humanity, because we have experienced God's love and compassion in that place, and so it becomes very natural for us to extend love and compassion to others in their humanity.

Right speech comes out of silence,

and right silence comes out of speech.

DIETRICH BONHOEFFER

For all of our piety and activity, we Christians are not always known for our kindness. Sometimes we are downright mean and judgmental. But most, if not all, of our meanness comes out of the places within us that have been unattended and untouched by God's love. Every broken place that has not been healed and transformed in God's presence is a hard edge of our personality that slices and dices other people when they bump up against it.

No wonder Bonhoeffer makes the startling and counterintuitive statement "Let him who cannot be alone beware of community." Without solitude we are dangerous in the human community and in the Christian community, because we are at the mercy of our compulsions, compelled by our inner emptiness into a self-oriented, anxious search for fullness in the next round of activities, accomplishments or relationships. When we are not finding ourselves loved by

God in solitude, in the company of others we are always on the prowl for ways they can fill our emptiness. We enter life in community trying to grab and grasp from others what only God can give.

On the other hand, when we are experiencing ourselves as the beloved of God, accepted and cherished by him in all of our beauty and brokenness, our hard, rough edges start to soften. We begin to see others as beloved as well, and that is what gets reflected back to them when they look into our eyes. Not only does the love of God come *to* us in solitude, the love of God begins to pour *through* us to others. This is a very different kind of productivity, and only God can bring it forth.

For me, productivity can no longer be measured solely by numbers of things—number of books written, number of new messages prepared and delivered, number of retreats led, number of people evangelized. Plenty of that is still happening, but that is no longer the way I measure success. Success for me now is measured by whether I am living within the rhythms of work and rest, solitude and community, silence and word necessary so the quality of my presence with God and with people and tasks is characterized by love and attention, wisdom and discernment. Success is knowing that the jar of river water is still finding time to sit still so the waters of my soul are clear enough to discern, to the best of my ability, what this moment calls for, and the next, and the next, and the next.

I have watched my life carefully enough to have a pretty good sense of how much time I need to spend in solitude and silence daily, weekly and monthly in order to stay grounded in God and for his love and wisdom to flow more consistently through my life. It has taken a number of years of exploring and experimenting for me to know what's needed to be truly well at the soul level, but I am now as clear about that as I am about knowing that I need to eat three meals a day.

These rhythms have become nonnegotiables in my life, but I don't hold to them legalistically. When they slip, I don't indulge in a guilt binge, I don't look to external motivators to find my way back, and I don't push harder on things that aren't working. Instead I just notice: Where has my desire gone? What have I gotten caught up in that has caused me to be out of touch with my desire and capacity to give God my undivided attention in solitude?

Then I give myself time and space to go back to the beginning, back to the place where this whole journey started for me: desperation and desire. I go back and find that place inside me that longs for more of God than what I have right now, more of truth than what I have right now, more authentic spiritual transformation than I have right now. I let my longings draw me back into the rhythms that sustain my life.

For there is nothing that fills like the Love that is God. There is nothing that transforms like the Presence that is God. There is nothing else that produces what the Silence of God produces within the human soul.

Catherine de Hueck Doherty writes that

> such silence is holy, a prayer beyond all prayers, leading to the final prayer of constant presence to God, to the heights of contemplation when the soul, finally at peace, lives by the will of him whom she loves totally, utterly, and completely. This silence, then, will break forth in a charity that overflows in the service of the neighbor without counting the cost. It will witness to Christ anywhere, always. Availability will become delightsome and easy, for in each person the soul will see the face of her Love. Hospitality will be deep and real, for a silent heart is a loving heart, and a loving heart is a hospice to the world.

Practice

As you enter into solitude and silence today, allow yourself to sit quietly for a time—ten minutes at least—and just enjoy the presence of the One who is always present with you. Notice how your capacity to be present to God has changed or shifted as you have entered into the practices of solitude and silence more intentionally.

After you have spent time just enjoying God's presence, invite him to show you a time or times in recent days when the quality of your presence with others has seemed different. Perhaps you experienced an increased capacity to feel and trust love in a particular relationship. Perhaps you experienced a flash of wisdom or discernment that you were courageous enough to follow, and you were surprised by the result. Perhaps you were self-aware enough to hold back a critical or manipulative comment and offer a more edifying one instead. Perhaps in a difficult moment you rested into God rather than reacting with panic.

Ask God to help you to notice what he wants you to notice. Allow yourself to savor the transformation that this incident represents in your life.

Now identify the rhythms of solitude and silence that were in place in your life that seemed to bring this good fruit. Based on all of your experiences with solitude and silence prior to and during your interactions with this book, begin exploring and identifying your own rhythms for solitude and silence. Be as concrete and realistic as possible. As you feel ready, tell God of your desire and your commitment.

Appendix

A DAY IN SOLITUDE:
BEING YOURSELF WITH GOD

Solitude, at its most basic and profound level, is simply an opportunity to be ourselves with God. When Elijah entered into his time of solitude, he had experienced a great deal of success, but it had taken its toll. He was physically exhausted, discouraged and in need of direction. His first step into solitude and silence was to stop, to acknowledge the truth about himself and to rest in God's presence. He made no attempt to sanitize anything, fix anything or judge anything. He was free to be himself—just as he was on that day—in God's presence.

This is our invitation as well. We, too, enter into solitude in the midst of life situations that affect the way we are with God and what it is we need to receive from him. Just as time spent together enables human friends to grow more and more comfortable with being themselves in each other's presence, extended periods of solitude give us the opportunity to enter more deeply into the experience of bringing our whole selves into relationship with God. The purpose of this retreat day is to help you be with God right where you are so that he can minister to you right where you are.

As you enter into your day of solitude, choose a place at home or in a retreat center environment that feels comfortable and safe to you, a place that allows you enough privacy to be open and available to God. Begin by settling into a comfortable position in your body and sitting quietly for a few moments, breathing deeply. Become aware of God's presence with you and your desire to be present with God on this day. After you have calmed and quieted your soul, tell God what you need and what you desire on this day. Write in your journal if that helps you to be more specific and concrete. You may want to reread Elijah's story in 1 Kings 19 as a way of settling into this set-apart time.

Notice whether or not you are physically tired, and if you are, allow yourself to do something that feels restful to you—take a nap, sit quietly in a chapel or lay on a blanket in the sun. You may need to rest for an hour or more; give yourself all the time you need to begin experiencing the restoration that will enable you to be alert in God's presence. As you give yourself to resting, be conscious of the fact that you are doing so at God's invitation.

When you have rested and as you feel ready, begin to notice what is true about you these days using the following questions as a guide. Take as much time as you need with each question, knowing that answering them fully and following God's invitations within them might take the whole day.

What is your physical condition lately? Are you tired, energized, satisfied with your level of health and fitness, eating well or not, caring for health issues and so on? Talk with God about these things and listen for his response.

What concerns and questions have been occupying your thoughts recently? How has your mind been working on these questions, and what is the result? On this day, spend time sitting in stillness with your question(s), or go for a slow, meditative walk carrying your question with you. Don't grasp for answers. Instead, remain in God's presence with your question in the spirit of Psalm 62:1: "In silence my soul waits for you and you alone, O God." See what happens.

What is the condition of your soul these days—what concerns are weighing on you? What joys or successes are you celebrating? Where do you hurt? Bring these to God today as a child would bring squeals of delight or tears of sadness or frustration to a loving parent. Allow yourself to experience everything that is true for you right now without censoring anything. Speak to God directly about what you are experiencing, and invite God to be with you in that place.

Reflections at the End of the Day

After Elijah had been in solitude for quite some time, God asked him again, "What are you doing here, Elijah?" It was a way of checking in to see, "So, how are you doing now?"

Elijah was still in a state that clearly indicated that he needed to make some changes in his life. In response to Elijah's condition, God graciously responded with some very specific instructions for his health and well-being as he returned to his normal activities (1 Kings 19:15-18). This guidance seemed to come not so much because Elijah asked for guidance but rather as a natural result of the fact that he had gotten quiet enough to hear.

So how are you doing now? Take a few moments at the close of this day to reflect on what happened between you and God during this time. Are there any shifts or changes that have taken place since you first entered into solitude? Is there anything that you know more clearly now than you did before you became quiet? Is there any guidance or invitation from God in this? How will you respond to God's invitation to you?

As you bring this day to a close, thank God for his presence with you throughout the day, and move gently and prayerfully back into your life in the company of others.

Sources

Chapter 1: Beyond Words
The quote from Gunilla Norris comes from *Sharing Silence* (New York: Bell Tower, 1992), pp. 13-14.

Chapter 2: Beginnings
M. Basil Pennington's words are found in *Centered Living* (New York: Doubleday, 1988), p. 56.

Richard Foster writes of the workings of spiritual disciplines in "Growing Edges," *Renovaré,* April 1999, p. 1.

William Shannon encourages us toward humble, wordless prayer in *Silence on Fire* (New York: Crossroad, 1991), p. 11.

Chapter 3: Resistance
Dallas Willard's insight into our fear of silence comes from *The Spirit of the Disciplines: Understanding How God Changes Lives* (San Francisco: HarperSanFrancisco, 1998), p. 163.

Carlo Carretto's words are from *The God Who Comes* (Maryknoll, N.Y.: Orbis, 1974).

Elizabeth Dreyer's paean to desire comes from *Earth Crammed with Heaven* (New York: Paulist, 1994), pp. 65-66.

Chapter 5: Rest for the Body

The anonymous woman's discoveries about her physical tension come from *Holy Meeting Ground: Twenty Years of Shalem,* comp. and ed. Connie Clark (Washington, D.C.: Shalem Institute, 1994), p. 50.

The meditation on honoring our body is found in Dorothy Bass, *Practicing Our Faith: A Way of Life for Searching People* (San Francisco: Jossey-Bass, 1997), pp. 14-15.

Chapter 6: Rest for the Mind

Henri Nouwen warns against overtaxing the mind in prayer in *The Way of the Heart* (San Francisco: HarperSanFrancisco, 1991), p. 74.

The "heart speaks to heart" reflection is also from Nouwen, *Way of the Heart,* p. 76.

Richard Rohr introduced this metaphor of the moon and the finger pointing to it in his book *Everything Belongs: The Gift of Contemplative Prayer* (New York: Crossroad, 1999), p. 46.

Rainer Marie Rilke's encouragement to patience is from *Letters to a Young Poet,* trans. M. D. Herter Norton (New York: W. W. Norton), p. 35.

Chapter 7: Rest for the Soul

Frederick Buechner speaks of the comfort of wordless prayer in "Telling Secrets," as quoted in *A Guide to Prayer for Ministers and Other Servants* (Nashville: Upper Room, 1983), p. 105.

The concept of the true self and the false self is a consistent theme not only in Scripture but also in the writings of the church fathers and mothers. Thomas Merton and Henri Nouwen (particularly Nouwen's *The Way of the Heart*) and Father Thomas Keating are contemporary authors who have shaped my understanding of this aspect of the spiritual life. Also, I am deeply indebted to my teaching partner

Dr. Rich Plass of The Transforming Center, from whom I have learned the language of the adaptive self. This is another way of identifying the false part of ourselves that relies on deeply patterned and often unconscious self-protective behaviors developed in response to the presence of sin and wounding within and around us. Spiritual transformation involves peeling back the layers of these adaptive responses in order to reveal the authentic self. Thus the process of transformation offers us the opportunity to live from a place of greater authenticity and the ability to be given over to God rather than being bound by the old self and its behaviors.

Chapter 9: Facing Ourselves

The words about the places where God meets and changes us are from M. Robert Mulholland, *Invitation to a Journey* (Downers Grove, Ill.: InterVarsity Press, 1993), p. 37.

The book on Christian community is titled *Equal to the Task: Men & Women in Partnership* (Downers Grove, Ill.: InterVarsity Press, 1998).

Chapter 10: Pure Presence

My explanation of biblical knowing relies on *Vine's Expository Dictionary of Old and New Testament Words,* ed. W. E. Vine, Merrill F. Unger and William White (Nashville: Nelson, 1985), p. 347.

The idea of communion beyond words is attributed to Thomas Merton.

Carl Arico defines transformation in *A Taste of Silence* (New York: Continuum, 1999), p. 29.

Chapter 11: Receiving Guidance

Thoughts on the first goal of the spiritual apprentice are by Dallas

Willard, *The Divine Conspiracy* (San Francisco: HarperSanFrancisco, 1998), p. 321.

Albert Edward Day explores the value of small steps of obedience in "The Captivating Presence," as quoted in *A Guide to Prayer for Ministers and Other Servants* (Nashville: Upper Room, 1983), p. 67.

The exercise at the end of the chapter is adapted from Dennis Linn, Sheila Fabricant Linn and Matthew Linn, *Sleeping with Bread: Holding What Gives You Life* (New York: Paulist, 1995), pp. 6-8.

Chapter 12: For the Sake of Others

Dietrich Bonhoeffer's words on speech and silence come from *Life Together,* trans. John W. Doberstein (New York: Harper, 1954), p. 78.

The final celebration of the gifts of silence comes in the words of Catherine de Hueck Doherty, *Poustinia: Christian Spirituality of the East for Western Man* (Notre Dame, Ind.: Ave Maria, 1975), p. 21.

Ruth Haley Barton is a teacher, spiritual director and retreat leader trained through the Shalem Institute for Spiritual Formation (Washington, D.C.) and The Pathways Center for Spiritual Leadership (Nashville). Ruth is cofounder of The Transforming Center, a community of Christian men and women who shape and care for the souls of leaders, equipping them to guide their churches and communities to become communities of spiritual transformation that discern and do the will of God in their setting.

Educated at Wheaton College and Northern Baptist Theological Seminary, Ruth has served on the pastoral staff of several churches, including Willow Creek Community Church as associate director of spiritual formation. Ruth lives with her husband, Chris, and their three daughters in Wheaton, Illinois. Her published works include

Equal to the Task: Men and Women in Partnership (InterVarsity Press)

An Ordinary Day with Jesus: Experiencing the Reality of God in Your Everyday Life (a spiritual formation curriculum coauthored with John Ortberg, Willow Creek Resources)

Ruth: Relationships That Bring Life (a Fisherman Bible Study, Shaw)

The Truths That Free Us: A Woman's Calling to Spiritual Transformation (Shaw)

For more information about The Transforming Center or Ruth's speaking schedule, please visit <www.thetransformingcenter.org>.